# A BIBLIOGRAPHY
# OF THE WORKS OF
# EUGENE O'NEILL

(No. 1)

*Pleiades Club Year Book for* 1912
*Containing poem,* "*Free*"

# A BIBLIOGRAPHY OF THE WORKS OF EUGENE O'NEILL

*together with*

# THE COLLECTED POEMS OF EUGENE O'NEILL

*compiled and edited by*

Ralph Sanborn and Barrett H. Clark

Benjamin Blom

*Printed in U.S.A. by*
NOBLE OFFSET PRINTERS, INC.
NEW YORK 3, N. Y.

# FOREWORD

THE impulse that leads men to compile accurate and complete lists of authors' writings is a curious thing: the collector and the dealer understand it, the author usually does not, and he who is the victim of it is driven by a variety of motives. An elaborate bibliography like the one you now hold in your hand is hardly the sort of thing that ministers to one's sense of pride as a "creative" writer, and neither this nor any other that I know has yielded any considerable monetary return. The profits, if any, accrue only to those shrewd or lucky purchasers who know what books to buy, and buy them at the right time.

A bibliography is usually, I think, a form of tribute. I cannot imagine how anyone would otherwise willingly explore the by-products, the experimental odds and ends and literary wild oats of any writer whose best work he positively disliked. There may, however, be exceptions, but the present work at any rate, with all its shortcomings, was undertaken in order to express our enthusiasm for the art of Mr. O'Neill and our unbounded respect for the consistent and uncompromising character of his uninterrupted labors during the seventeen years of his career as a writer. We have followed not only his development as a maker of plays, we have gone out of our way to trace the most inconsequential of his efforts to their ultimate sources and record them side by side with his best-known publications. We have, like all bibliographers who know what is expected of them and rejoice in the pursuit for its own sake, come to regard even the unconsidered trifles of our author with a certain paternal affection. The excitement of the chase, the joy of capture and the satisfaction of exhibiting the trophy — such things are among the rewards of bibliographers.

It is the bibliographer's duty to record even the outcasts among a writer's products, the mistakes, the unsuccessful efforts in the long course of his evolution. That this is necessary and desirable is one of the prices that any writer of distinction must pay, for the iniquity of oblivion is visited only upon those who deserve it. Mr. O'Neill cannot escape the prowling bibliographer: indeed, after what he must have known was a vain attempt to avoid him (the him being my collaborator and me), he graciously bowed to the inevitable and himself joined us in the task of unearthing certain wholly forgotten juvenilia, items that had escaped even the vigilant eye of Mr. Sanborn, whose flair for such things amazes me.

In justice to Mr. O'Neill, therefore, it must be made clear that the early verse described in this book, and the examples reprinted, as well as the story *To-morrow*, are strictly outside the canon. They belong here as integral parts of a whole, that whole being the writings of Eugene O'Neill.

While our heaviest debt is to him, we gladly acknowledge valuable assistance from Mr. Albert H. Gross, of the staff of Horace Liveright, Inc.; to Mr. Frank Shay; to Mr. Frederick W. Edgerton, Librarian, of the Public Library at New London, Conn.; to the late George H. Sargent, the distinguished bibliographer; and to Mrs. Flora V. Livingston, author of the well-known Kipling bibliography.

In preparing the exact form of our work we have not hesitated to follow the arrangements of several other similar lists; to their authors, without detailed particularization, we thus publicly tender our thanks.

Since acknowledgments belong in this place and this short note appears over my signature alone, I hereby refuse to claim more than a small share in the work that follows. To Mr. Sanborn fell the task of doing most of it. I would gladly take half the credit if I honestly could.

Finally, it is perhaps not superfluous to say that no perfect bibliography has ever been compiled, and we realize that ours leaves something to be desired. It was our intention to learn all the pertinent facts, and for that reason we shall welcome whatever emendations anyone has to suggest. It is well, though, to state here that we have not thought it worth while to record translations of our author's work; to make *complete* lists of references on it; or to take cognizance of the reviews of productions of the plays.

BARRETT H. CLARK

20 April, 1931

# LIST OF
# ILLUSTRATIONS

PAGE

Pleiades Club Year Book for 1912 . . . facing title page

Title Page of Pleiades Club Year Book . . . . . . 2

Title Page of *Thirst* . . . . . . . . . . . 6

Front Cover of The Provincetown Plays—3rd Series . 11

Front Cover of first separate edition of *Before Breakfast* . 13

The Seven Arts Magazine for June, 1917 . . . facing 15

Title Page of *The Moon of the Caribbees* . . . . . 18

Title Page of *Beyond the Horizon* . . . . . . . 24

Theatre Arts Magazine for January, 1921 . . . facing 27

Title Page of *The Emperor Jones, Diff'rent, The Straw* . 29

Title Page of First Separate Edition of *Anna Christie* . . 39

First and Second Issues of *The Moon of The Caribbees*
facing 42

The Smart Set Magazine for August, 1918 . . facing 46

Title Page of Uniform Trade Edition of Collected Plays 52

First and Second Issue of *Beyond The Horizon* . facing 57

First and Second Issue of *The Emperor Jones, Diff'rent,*
*The Straw* . . . . . . . . . . . facing 65

Specimen page of Act One, *Lazarus Laughed* in The
American Caravan . . . . . . . . . . 68

Specimen page of Act One, *Lazarus Laughed* in the First
Edition . . . . . . . . . . . . . 69

Title Page of Limited Edition of *Strange Interlude* . . 74

Front cover of pamphlet, Extracts from *Strange Interlude*
facing 76

Specimen page of the English Edition of *Dynamo* . . . 80

Specimen page of the American Edition of Dynamo . . 81

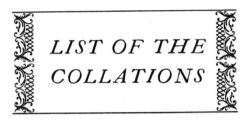

# LIST OF THE COLLATIONS

| Year | | Item No. |
|---|---|---|
| 1912 | Pleiades Club Book – "Free" – A poem | 1 |
| 1912 | New London Telegraph – Various poems | 2 |
| 1914 | New York Call – "Fratricide" – A poem | 3 |
| 1914 | Thirst – First Edition | 4 |
| 1915 | New York Tribune–"Speaking of Beatrices"–A poem | 5 |
| 1916 | Bound East For Cardiff – Provincetown Plays (1st Series) – First Edition | 6 |
| 1916 | Before Breakfast – Provincetown Plays (3rd Series) – First Edition | 7 |
| 1916 | – First Separate Edition | 8 |
| 1917 | The Masses – "Submarine" – A poem | 9 |
| 1917 | The Seven Arts – "Tomorrow" – A short story | 10 |
| 1917 | The Smart Set – "The Long Voyage Home" | 11 |
| 1918 | The Smart Set – "Ile" | 12 |
| 1918 | The Moon of the Caribbees – The Smart Set | 13 |
| 1919 | – First Edition with "Six Other Plays of the Sea" | 14 |
| 1923 | – English Edition | 15 |

| | | |
|---|---|---|
| 1920 | The Dreamy Kid – Theatre Arts Magazine | 16 |
| 1922 | – "Contemporary One-Act Plays of 1921" | 17 |
| 1920 | Beyond the Horizon – First Edition | 18 |
| 1924 | – English Edition | 19 |
| 1920 | New York Times – Letter from O'Neill | 20 |
| 1921 | – Letter from O'Neill about "Anna Christie" | 21 |
| 1921 | The Emperor Jones – Theatre Arts Magazine | 22 |
| 1921 | – First Edition with "Diff'rent" and "The Straw" | 23 |
| 1922 | – English Edition | 24 |
| 1921 | – First Separate Edition | 25 |
| 1925 | – Separate English Edition | 26 |
| 1928 | – Illustrated Edition | 27 |
| 1921 | Gold – First Edition | 28 |
| 1922 | The Hairy Ape, "Anna Christie", the First Man – First Edition | 29 |
| 1923 | – English Edition | 30 |
| 1923 | – "Anna Christie" – Separate Edition | 31 |
| 1929 | – "The Hairy Ape" – Illustrated Edition | 32 |
| 1930 | – "Anna Christie" – Illustrated Edition | 33 |
| 1923 | Provincetown PlayBill – "Strindberg, etc." | 34 |
| 1924 | – Sketches for "Desire, etc." | 35 |
| 1925 | – "Are The Actors to Blame?" | 36 |
| 1924 | All God's Chillun Got Wings – The American Mercury | 37 |
| 1924 | – First Edition with "Welded" | 38 |
| 1925 | – English Edition with "Desire Under the Elms" | 39 |
| 1924 | Greenwich PlayBill – Sketches for "Desire, etc." | 40 |
| 1925 | – Note by O'Neill | 41 |

| | | |
|---|---|---|
| 1925 | Collected Plays – Limited Edition – Volume I | 42 |
| 1925 | – Volume II with first edition of "Desire Under the Elms" | 43 |
| 1925 | Desire Under the Elms – First Separate Edition | 44 |
| 1925 | The Works of Eugene O'Neill – "Anna Christie", "All God's Chillun Got Wings", and "Diff'rent" | 45 |
| 1925 | – "Beyond the Horizon," "The Straw" and "Before Breakfast" | 46 |
| 1925 | – "Desire Under the Elms", "The Hairy Ape", and "Welded" | 47 |
| 1925 | – "The Emperor Jones", "Gold", "The First Man" and "The Dreamy Kid" | 48 |
| 1925 | The Boston Evening Transcript – "Playwright and Critic, etc." by Isaac Goldberg with letters from O'Neill | 49 |
| 1926 | New York Evening Post – "Eugene O'Neill Writes About His Latest Play" | 50 |
| 1926 | – "O'Neill Talks About 'Beyond the Horizon'". | 51 |
| 1929 | – Sketches for "Dynamo" | 52 |
| 1926 | The Great God Brown and The Fountain – First Edition | 53 |
| 1926 | – English Edition | 54 |
| 1926 | – "The Great God Brown" – First Separate Edition | 55 |
| 1926 | "Eugene O'Neill" – (B. H. Clark) – First Edition with letters, etc., from O'Neill | 56 |
| 1929 | – Revised Edition | 57 |
| 1927 | Marco Millions – First Edition | 58 |
| 1927 | – English Edition | 59 |
| 1927 | – Limited Edition | 60 |

1927 "A History of the American Drama" – (A. H. Quinn) – First Edition with letters from O'Neill 61

1927 Lazarus Laughed – American Caravan – First Edition of First Act 62

1927 – First Edition of Complete Play 63

1927 – Limited Edition 64

1928 Strange Interlude – First Edition 65

1928 – Limited Edition 66

1928 – English Edition 67

1929 – "Extracts from 'The Strange Interlude'". 68

1928 "Anathema" – (B. DeCasseres) – First Edition with Foreword by O'Neill 69

1929 New York World – Sketches for "Dynamo" 70

1929 Dynamo – First Edition 71

1929 – English Edition with "Lazarus Laughed" 72

– Limited Edition 73

# PART ONE

# COLLATIONS

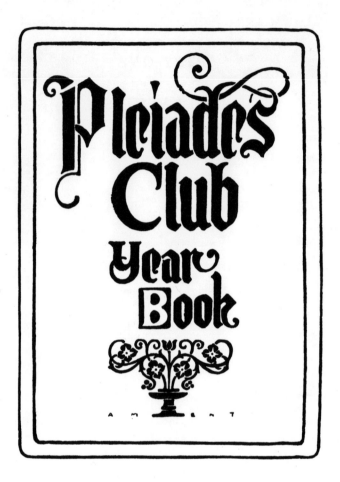

(No. 1)

*Title-page of book containing the poem "Free,"*
*the author's first published work*

## O'NEILL
## BIBLIOGRAPHY

I

## PLEIADES CLUB YEAR BOOK
## FREE

Pleiades / Club / Year / Book / [ornament in red] / [1912]

[All of which is enclosed by a single line black border within a single line red border. The "P" of Pleiades and the "C" of Club are in red and all of the lettering is of ornamental design.]

*See facsimile p. 2.*

Collation: 12mo. [leaf measures 6⅞ x 4⅞ inches]; pp. 144, consisting of; pp. [1-2], blank; p. [3], Title-page as above; p. [4], blank; p. [5], Certificate of issue — "This · Edition · De · Luxe · is · Limited / To · Five · Hundred · Copies / of · which · this · is / No. ———"; p. [6], contains, "Published in the Year / Eighteen of the / Pleiades / [Club insignia in red] / Copyright 1912 by the / Pleiades Club / N. Y. / All rights reserved"; p. [7],

List of Contributors with caption in red; p. [8], blank; pp. 9-
141, Text including reproductions in red of original illustrations; p. 142, List of Club Officers for 1911-1912; p. [143],
blank; p. [144], contains printer's card in lower left-hand
corner, "Printed by / Shultis- / Dudley / Company / New York."

Issued in full gray suede binding with buckle on front cover
and strap on back cover which holds book at the middle. Lettered in upper left-hand corner of front cover in gilt, "Pleiades."
Spine is blank. Edges are cut, and top edge is gilded. End papers
are mottled, antique decorated from left to right with parading
muses in pale green.

Published in April, 1912.
Edition limited to 500 copies.

Poem entitled "Free" by Eugene G. O'Neill appears on page 120
of the Pleiades Year Book. It has been designated by the author as
his first published work. It has not been previously collected but appears again here on page 111.

Copies of this volume were distributed to members and friends of
the Pleiades Club and were not for sale to the public.

*See illustration opposite title-page.*

## 2

# NEW LONDON TELEGRAPH

Poems contributed by Eugene O'Neill to a column
entitled "Laconics" appearing in the New London
Telegraph, a week-day newspaper formerly published in New London, Connecticut.

Issues which contained contributions in the column on the
editorial page during 1912 are as follows:

August 26, 27, 28, September 2, 6, 11, 13, 17, 23, 27, 28, October 3, 16, 17, 19, 22, 28, November 4, 5, 19, 21, 22, 27, and December 9.

These poems are collected here for the first time and are to be found on pp. 121-161.

It is probable that O'Neill made other contributions to this column, but the poems listed are all signed and thus are definitely known to be the author's work.

## 3

## NEW YORK CALL

A long poem entitled "Fratricide," located on p. 10 of the New York Call, a newspaper formerly published daily in New York City, issue for May 17, 1914.

This has not been previously collected.

*See p.* 113.

## 4

## THIRST

American Dramatists Series / Thirst / And other One Act Plays by / Eugene G. O'Neill / [Publisher's Device] / Boston: The Gorham Press / Toronto: The Copp Clark Co. Limited / [1914]

[All of which is enclosed by a single line border.]

*See facsimile p.* 6.

Collation: 12mo. [leaf measures 7⅜ x 4⅞ inches]; pp. 168, consisting of; p. [1], Title-page as above; p. [2], contains, "Copyright, 1914, by Eugene G. O'Neill / [short line] / Dra-

*American Dramatists Series*

# THIRST

*And Other One Act Plays by*

## EUGENE G. O'NEILL

ARTI et VERITATI

## BOSTON: THE GORHAM PRESS
### TORONTO: THE COPP CLARK CO., LIMITED

(No. 5)
*Title-page of author's first book*

matic and all Other Rights Reserved / The Gorham Press,
Boston, U. S. A."; p. [3], Table of Contents; p. [4], blank;
p. [5], Half-title, "Thirst / A Play in One Act / Characters /
A Gentleman / A Dancer / A West Indian Mulatto Sailor";
p. [6], blank; pp. 7-168, Text, containing the one act plays,
"Thirst," "The Web," "Warnings," "Fog," and "Recklessness."

Issued in dark grey boards with buff paper label pasted on
cover containing in brown print—"American Dramatists Series
/ Thirst / And other One Act Plays / [short double line] /
Eugene G. O'Neill," all boxed by thin double line. Spine is buff
cloth on which is pasted buff paper label containing in brown
print, "American Dramatists Series—Thirst—O'Neill."Edges
are cut. End papers are plain white. Issued with cream colored
dust wrapper.

First Published in August, 1914.
First Printing consisted of 1000 copies.

These are the first published plays by the author. They have not
been collected in full or in part and the author insists that they never
will be reprinted with his permission. Only one edition was printed
and the type subsequently distributed.

Errors for identification:

P. 54, l. 2 — Apostrophe is missing before "cause."
P. 98, l. 27 — Final parenthesis is missing after "piteously."
P. 115, l. 9 — Hyphen is missing at end of the line.
P. 159, l. 19 — "Astonished" has exaggerated spacing and the
"d" is not in italics.

# 5

# NEW YORK TRIBUNE

A poem, entitled "Speaking, to the Shade of Dante,
of Beatrices," composed of twenty-five lines and

located in F. P. A.'s "The Conning Tower" on p.
7 of the New York Tribune, a daily newspaper formerly published in New York City, issue for July
5, 1915.

It is signed, "E. O'N."
This has not been previously collected.

*See p.* 118.

## 6

## THE PROVINCETOWN PLAYS—

## FIRST SERIES

## BOUND EAST FOR CARDIFF

The / Provincetown / Plays / First Series: / Bound
East for Cardiff: Eugene G. O'Neill / The Game:
Louise Bryant / King Arthur's Socks: Floyd Dell /
New York / Frank Shay / 1916

Collation: 12mo. [leaf measures 8 x 5¼ inches]; pp. 67,
consisting of; p. [1], Half-title, "The Provincetown Plays /
First Series"; p. [2], blank; p. [3], Title-page as above; p.
[4], contains, "Copyright, 1915 by Louise Bryant. / Copyright, 1916 by Eugene G. O'Neill. / Copyright, 1916 by Floyd
Dell. / Copyright, 1916 by Frank Shay." / [Following which is
the permission clause enclosed in a single-line box] "Application for permission to perform these plays / may be made to
the Provincetown Players, 139 / Macdougal Street, New York;
no performance can / take place without arrangement with the
owners of / the acting rights."; p. [5], Half-title, "Bound East
for Cardiff / A Sea Play / By Eugene G. O'Neill"; p. [6], con-

tains program of play as presented at the Playwright's Theatre, New York City, November 1916; pp. 7-25, Text of "Bound East for Cardiff"; p. [26], blank; pp. [27]-67, Text of "The Game" and "King Arthur's Socks"; p. [68], blank.

Issued in blue wrappers, lettered in dark blue on front cover, "The · Provincetown · Plays · / First Series: / Bound East for Cardiff: Eugene G. O'Neill / The Game: Louise Bryant / King Arthur's Socks: Floyd Dell / [original wood-block illustration by William Zorach] / Frank Shay, Publisher 1916." Lettered in dark blue on spine, "The Provincetown Plays — First Series." Back cover contains advertisement of the Washington Square Book Shop. All edges are uncut and end papers are plain white.

First published in November, 1916.
First printing contained 1200 copies.

Most of the copies of this first printing were distributed gratis to writers, actors and others associated with or interested in the Playwrights' Theatre. Some copies were sold at the theatre during the intermissions.

Errors for identification:

    P. 12, l. 24 — "lays" is incorrect.
        Changed to "lies" in Moon of the Caribbees No. 14.

    P. 16, l. 4 — The name Ivan should start the line as that stage direction and speech are his and not Smitty's as indicated.

    P. 25, l. 13-14 — Should all be in italics.

*See also No. 14.*

## BEFORE BREAKFAST

### 7

## THE PROVINCETOWN PLAYS— THIRD SERIES

### FIRST EDITION

The / Provincetown / Plays / Third Series: / The Two Sons: Neith Boyce / Lima Beans: Alfred Kreymborg/Before Breakfast: Eugene O'Neill/ New York / Frank Shay / 1916

Collation: 12mo. [leaf measures 8 x 5¼ inches]; pp. 141-208, consisting of; p. [141], Half-title, "The Provincetown Plays/Third Series"; p. [142], blank; p. [143], Title-page as above; p. [144], contains, "Copyright, 1916, by Eugene G. O'Neill./Copyright, 1916, by Alfred Kreymborg./Copyright, 1916 by Neith Boyce."/ [Following which is the permission clause enclosed in a single-line box] "Application for permission to perform these plays / may be made to the Provincetown Players, 17 West / Eighth Street, New York; no performance can take / place without arrangement with the owners of the / acting rights."; p. [145] Half-title, "The Two Sons/A Play in One Act / By Neith Boyce"; pp. 145-191, Text of "The Two Sons" and "Lima Beans"; p. [192], blank; p. [193], Half-title, "Before Breakfast /A Play in One Act / By Eugene G. O'Neill"; p. [194], contains program of play as presented by the Provincetown Players, New York City, December 1916; pp. 195-207, Text of "Before Breakfast"; p. [208], blank.

Issued in orange wrappers, lettered in black on front cover,

# ·THE·PROVINCETOWN·PLAYS·

## THIRD SERIES:

The Two Sons: *Neith Boyce*

Lima Beans: *Alfred Kreymborg*

Before Breakfast: *Eugene G. O'Neill*

**FRANK SHAY,** *Publisher* **1916**

(No. 7)

*Reproduction of front cover*

" · The · Provincetown · Plays · /Third Series:/The Two Sons:
Neith Boyce / Lima Beans: Alfred Kreymborg / Before Breakfast: Eugene G. O'Neill / [original wood-block illustration by
William Zorach, uniform with "The Provincetown Plays —
First Series" No. 6] /Frank Shay, Publisher 1916." *See facsimile p* 11. Lettered in black on spine, "The Provincetown
Plays — Third Series." Back cover contains advertisement of
the Washington Square Book Shop. All edges are uncut and
end papers are plain white.

First published December, 1916.
First printing consisted of 500 copies.

The publisher of this book reports that some copies were later issued
but without the imprint "Frank Shay, Publisher 1916" appearing on
the front cover.

The Provincetown Plays Series were paginated in sequence which
explains the higher pagination in this volume — the third.

Errors for identification:

     P. 196 — Last paragraph should be in italics.
     P. 198, l. 23 — First word in the line should be "on" and
         not "of" as given.
     P. 200, l. 14 — The word "it" should be inserted after
         "waste."

*See also No. 8.*

# 8

### FIRST SEPARATE EDITION

## Before Breakfast / A Play in One Act / By Eugene G. O'Neill / New York / Frank Shay / 1916

Collation: 12mo. [leaf measures $7\frac{7}{8}$ x $5\frac{1}{4}$ inches]; pp. 24,
consisting of; p. [1], Half-title, "Before Breakfast"; p. [2],
blank; p. [3], Title-page as above; p. [4], contains, "Copyright 1916, by Eugene G. O'Neill / [and enclosed in single-line

# BEFORE BREAKFAST *a*
*Play in One Act by Eugene G. O'Neill*

**FRANK SHAY, *Publisher* 1916**

(No. 8)

*Reproduction of front cover
of first separate edition*

box] All dramatic rights reserved / by the author"; p. [5],
Half-title, "Before Breakfast / A Play in One Act / By Eugene
G. O'Neill"; p. [6], contains program of play as presented by
the Provincetown Players, New York City in December, 1916;
pp. 7-19, Text of the play; pp. [20-24], blank.

Issued in light blue wrappers, lettered in black on front cover,
"Before Breakfast a / Play in One Act by Eugene G. O'Neill /
Frank Shay, Publisher 1916". *See facsimile p.* 13. Back cover
contains advertisement of Washington Square Book Shop, but
in contrast to the back cover of "The Provincetown Plays —
Third Series" No. 7 the shop is identified as the property of
Frank Shay and the new address of 17 West 8th Street is given.
Top edge is cut, other edges are uncut and unopened. No end
papers.

First published in December, 1916.
First printing consisted of 500 copies.

This issue was prepared from the text and type of "The Provincetown Plays — Third Series" No. 7, the front matter and pagination
being revised. All errors in former are common in this issue.

The publisher states that this issue was published several days after
"The Provincetown Plays — Third Series" No. 7.

# 9

## THE MASSES

An unsigned poem, entitled, "Submarine," composed of sixteen lines and located on p. 43 of "The
Masses", a magazine formerly published monthly
in New York City, issue for February, 1917.

This has not been previously collected.

*See p.* 120.

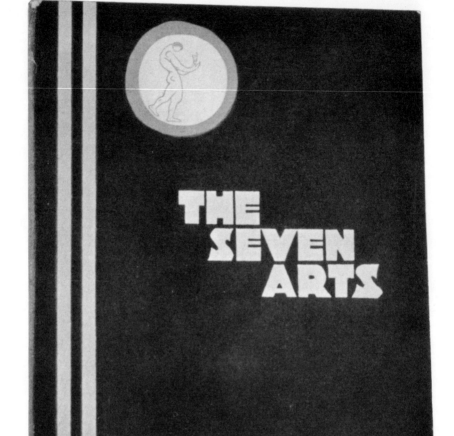

(No. 10)

*Contains short story, "Tomorrow"*

## 10

# THE SEVEN ARTS
# TOMORROW

The Seven Arts, a magazine formerly published monthly in New York City, issue for June, 1917 [Vol. 2, No. 8].

Collation: 8vo. [leaf measures 9⅝ x 6₁₆⁷ inches]; pp. vii+ 133-260; pp. 147-170 contain short story "Tomorrow" by Eugene G. O'Neill.

Issued in dark blue wrappers. Front cover contains two parallel orange stripes running length of left side, orange seal design at upper left center, "The / Seven / Arts" in light blue at right center and "The War and the Intellectuals/By Randolph Bourne/June, 1917/25 Cents" in yellow at bottom.

This is an uncollected story. The item is of particular importance because of its very personal nature the author forbids any reprinting of it and because it is the only short story which has been published by the author.

*See illustration opposite.*

## 11

# THE SMART SET
# THE LONG VOYAGE HOME

The Smart Set, a magazine published monthly in New York City, issue for October, 1917 [Vol. 53, No. 2].

Collation: 8vo. [leaf measures 9¹⅜ x 6¾ inches]; pp. iv+ 144; pp. 83-94 contain one-act play, "The Long Voyage Home" by Eugene G. O'Neill.

Issued in wrappers. Front cover is gray with uniform title of "The/Smart/Set/A Magazine of/Cleverness" in red at top and with illustration of girl.

This play was subsequently collected in "The Moon of the Caribbees" No. 14.

## 12

# THE SMART SET

## ILE

The Smart Set, a magazine published monthly in New York City, issue for May, 1918 [Vol. 55, No. 1].

Collation: 8vo. [leaf measures 9¹⅜ x 6¾ inches]; pp. iv+ 144; pp. 89-100 contain one-act play, "Ile" by Eugene G. O'Neill.

Issued in wrappers uniform with No. 11 except for illustration of girl.

This play was subsequently collected in "The Moon of the Caribbees" No. 14.

# THE MOON OF THE CARIBBEES
## 1918-1923
## 13
## THE SMART SET

The Smart Set, a magazine published monthly in New York City, issue for August, 1918 [Vol. 55, No. 4].

Collation: 8vo. [leaf measures $9\frac{13}{16}$ x 6¾ inches]; pp. iv+ 144; pp. 73-86, contain one-act play, "The Moon of the Caribbees" by Eugene G. O'Neill.

Issued in wrappers uniform with No. 11 except for illustration of girl.

This play was subsequently collected as the title play in "The Moon of the Caribbees" No. 14.

*See illustration p. 46.*

## 14

### FIRST EDITION

## THE MOON OF THE CARIBBEES
## AND SIX OTHER PLAYS OF THE SEA

The Moon of/the Caribbees/and/Six other Plays of the Sea/By/Eugene G. O'Neill/[Publisher's Device]/Boni and Liveright/New York 1919

*See facsimile p. 18.*

# THE MOON OF THE CARIBBEES

AND

## SIX OTHER PLAYS OF THE SEA

BY

## EUGENE G. O'NEILL

## BONI AND LIVERIGHT
## NEW YORK          1919

(No. 14)

*Title-page of the first edition*

Collation: 12mo. [leaf measures $7\frac{5}{16}$ x $5\frac{1}{8}$ inches]; pp. vi+ 218, consisting of; p. [1], Half-title, "The Moon of the Caribbees/and Six other Plays of the Sea"; p. [ii], blank; p. [iii], Title-page as above; p. [iv], contains, "Copyright, 1919,/By Boni & Liveright, Inc."; p. [5], Table of Contents; p. [vi], blank; p. [1], Half-title, "The Moon of the Caribbees / A Play in One Act"; p. [2], List of Characters; pp. 3-217, Text of the one act plays, "The Moon of the Caribbees," "Bound East for Cardiff," "The Long Voyage Home," "In the Zone," "Ile," "Where the Cross is Made" and "The Rope"; p. [218], blank.

Issued in cinnamon brown boards lettered on front cover in black, "The Moon/of The/Caribbees/Eugene G. O'Neill." Spine is tan cloth lettered in black, "The Moon/of The Caribbees / Eugene G. / O'Neill / Boni and / Liveright". Top edges are cut, others uncut and unopened. End papers are plain. Issued with orange and yellow dust wrapper.

First published in June, 1919.
First printing consisted of 1200 copies.

"The Moon of the Caribbees" first appeared in the Smart Set, August, 1918. See No. 13.

"The Long Voyage Home" first appeared in the Smart Set, October, 1917. See No. 11.

"Ile" first appeared in the Smart Set, May, 1918. See No. 12.

"Bound East for Cardiff" appeared in 1916. See No. 6.

The first issue differs from subsequent issues in point of size. The second issue has leaves which measure $7\frac{7}{16}$ x $5\frac{1}{16}$. Furthermore, in thickness the second issue measures $1\frac{3}{16}''$ overall whereas the first issue only measures $\frac{7}{8}''$. An important presentation copy substantiates this contention. Also, if it is possible to compare the original dust wrappers of the first and second issues it will be seen that only 68 volumes of the Modern Library have been listed on the smaller wrapper of the first issue, whereas 88 are listed on the larger wrapper of the second issue. In point of binding both issues seem to be uniform.

Consequently, it is obvious that the first issue (number of copies comprising same is not known) was a distinctly different book from the second issue.

*See illustration p. 42.*

There are innumerable editorial changes in the texts of "Moon of the Caribbees," "The Long Voyage Home," and "Ile" as compared to the original printing of these plays in The Smart Set. The chief variation is the presence in this volume of profanity and coarser language than appeared in the magazines. "Bound East for Cardiff" has also been edited as reprinted from its original printing in the Provincetown Plays — 1st Series.

Errors for identification:

P. 30, l. 5 & 8 — These two lines should be continuous. The latter line is obviously misplaced.

P. 108, l. 4 — Should be "no" instead of "now."

P. 128, l. 20 — Has "no'th'ard" but elsewhere (e.g. p. 119, l. 21) has "no'the'ard."

These errors — and others of minor consequence which are not included here — are common to all issues and printings of this volume.

*See also No.* 6, 11, 12 and 13.

# 15

### ENGLISH EDITION

The Moon of the Caribbees / And Six Other Plays of the Sea / by Eugene G. O'Neill / [Publisher's Device] / With an Introduction by / St. John Ervine / Jonathan Cape / Eleven Gower Street, London / [1923]

Collation: Crown 8vo; pp. 237 — each play having separate pagination.

Issued in bright blue cloth, no printing on front cover but with white title label pasted on spine. Issued in cream dust wrapper.

First published in April, 1923.

Plays are the same and in the same order as in the American Edition No. 14. In addition, however, this volume has an eleven page introduction by St. John Ervine.

# THE DREAMY KID

## 1920-1922

## 16

## THEATRE ARTS MAGAZINE

Theatre Arts Magazine, published monthly in New York City, issue for January, 1920 [Vol. 4, No. 1].

Collation: 8vo. [leaf measures 9½ x 6⅜ inches]; pp. 88 [pp. 7 & 8 - 81 & 82 omitted in the pagination. Text is complete]; pp. [41]-56, contain one-act play, "The Dreamy Kid" by Eugene G. O'Neill.

Issued in cream-colored wrappers. Front cover contains in brown, "Theatre Arts / Magazine / [Illustration] / Volume IV — Number 1 / January, 1920."

Errors for identification:
　　P. 49, l. 11 — Should be "again" instead of "agin."
　　P. 54, l. 7 — Bracket should follow "roughly" instead of precede "Come."
This play was subsequently collected in an anthology of plays edited by Frank Shay and entitled, "Contemporary One-Act Plays of 1921" No. 17.

## 17

FIRST EDITION

# CONTEMPORARY ONE-ACT PLAYS
## OF 1921

Contemporary/One-Act Plays/of 1921/(American)/Selected and Edited by/Frank Shay/[Publisher's Device]/Cincinnati/Stewart Kidd Company/Publishers/[1922]

Collation: 8vo. [leaf measures 8 x 5$\frac{7}{16}$ inches]; pp. ii+630, consisting of; p. [i], Half-title, "Contemporary One-Act Plays / of 1921 / (American)"; p. [ii], blank; p. [1], Title-page as above; p. [2], contains 'Copyright, 1922 / Stewart Kidd Company / [Publishers Device] / All rights reserved / Printed in the United States of America / The Caxton Press / "Everybody for Books". This is one of the Interlacken Library'; p. [3] Dedication, "To / Eugene O'Neill"; pp. 5-6, Foreword by Editor; p. [7], Table of Contents; p. [8], blank; p. [9], Half-title; p. [10], blank; pp. 11-630 Text of the plays with "The Dreamy Kid" by Eugene O'Neill pp. [487]-517.

Issued in green cloth, lettered in gold on front cover, "Contemporary / One-Act / Plays / [short line] / 1921 / [short line] / American / Edited by / Frank Shay / [small design]". All of which is enclosed in a double-line gold box. Spine is lettered in gold, "Contemporary/One-Act / Plays / [short line] / 1921 / [short line] / American / [short line] / Shay / [small design] / Stewart / Kidd". Edges are cut, and end papers are plain. Top edges are stained red.

First published in October, 1922.
First printing consisted of 2000 copies.

The text as given in this volume has many editorial changes as compared to the first printing of the play in the Theatre Arts Magazine, January, 1920. See No. 16.

The title of later editions of this volume was changed to "Twenty Contemporary One-Act Plays."

*See also No.* 16.

# BEYOND THE HORIZON

## 1920-1924

## 18

### FIRST EDITION

Beyond the Horizon / A Play in Three Acts / By / Eugene G. O'Neill / [Publisher's Device] / Boni and Liveright / Publishers New York / [1920]

*See facsimile p.* 24.

Collation: 12mo. [leaf measures $7\frac{1}{2}$ x $5\frac{1}{16}$ inches]; pp. x+166, consisting of; p. [i], Half-title, "Beyond the Horizon"; p. [ii], contains "Plays by / Eugene G. O'Neill / [single-line] / The Moon of the Caribbees / and Six Other Plays of the Sea / Chris Christopherson" [all of which is contained in a single line box]; p. [iii], Title-page as above; p. [iv], contains, "Copyright, 1920, / by Boni & Liveright, Inc. / Printed in the United States of America"; p. [v], Dedication, "To Agnes"; p. [vi], blank; p. [vii] List of Acts and Scenes; p. [viii], blank; p. [ix], Half-title, "Act I"; p. [x], List of Characters; pp. 1-165 Text of the three-act play; p. 166, blank.

# BEYOND THE HORIZON

## A PLAY IN THREE ACTS

BY

## EUGENE G. O'NEILL

## BONI AND LIVERIGHT
## PUBLISHERS    NEW YORK

(No. 18)

*Title-page of the first edition*

Issued in cinnamon brown — or muddy brown — boards lettered on front cover in black, "Beyond/the/Horizon/Eugene G. O'Neill". Spine is tan cloth lettered in black, "Beyond/the /Horizon/Eugene G./O'Neill/Boni and/Liveright". Top edges are cut, others uncut and unopened. End papers are plain. Issued with orange and yellow dust wrapper.

First published in March, 1920.
First printing consisted of 1250 copies.

The first issue differs from subsequent issues in point of binding. It is uniform in materials and size with the later issues of "Moon of the Caribbees" inasmuch as it was to be a part of the uniform series started by the latter publication No. 14. However, after the first issue of "Beyond the Horizon" had been bound and distributed the subsequent issues were bound in lighter colored and different textured materials and leaf measure is $7\frac{3}{8}"$ x $5\frac{1}{16}"$.

Also, printing on cover varied. In first issue upper case letters of title measure $\frac{9}{16}$ of an inch, lower case letters measure $\frac{3}{8}$ of an inch, and upper case letters of author's name measure $\frac{3}{8}$ of an inch and lower case letters measure $\frac{1}{4}$ of an inch. As seen in illustration, style of type varies in author's name.

*See illustration p. 57.*

The identity of the first issue has been substantiated by an important presentation copy which is dated March 28, 1920.

Errors for identification:

      P. 18, l. 8 — Should be "grimace" instead of "grimac."

      P. 26, l. 25 — "Takes his" at end of line should be in italics.

      P. 41, l. 13 — Should be "kissing" instead of "kising."

      P. 49, l. 9 — Should be "tone" instead of "one."

      P. 86, l. 30 — Should be "Besides" instead of "Besies."

      P. 139, l. 13 — Should be "mournfully" instead of "mornfully."

It should be noted that the errors given above appeared in all issues and printings of this volume. They appear in a printing made in 1923.

## 19

Beyond the Horizon / and Gold two plays / by / Eugene O'Neill / [Publisher's Device] / Jonathan Cape Ltd / Eleven Gower Street, London / [1924]

Collation: Crown 8vo.; pp. viii+304, each play having separate pagination.

Issued in bright blue cloth, no printing on front cover, but with white title label pasted on spine. Issued in cream colored dust wrapper.

First published in April, 1924.

These two plays were published separately in American editions.

*Uniform with No.* 15.

## NEW YORK TIMES

### 1920-1924

### 20

Letter from O'Neill to the New York Times, a daily newspaper published in New York City, on p. 2, Section 6 of the issue for April 11, 1920.

# THEATRE ARTS
# MAGAZINE

VOLUME V — NUMBER 1
JANUARY 1921

(No. 22)

*Contains first printing of "The Emperor Jones"*

## 21

Letter entitled, "From Eugene O'Neill" concerning "Anna Christie" and sent from Provincetown, Mass., December 12, 1921, on p. 1, Section 6 of the issue for December 18, 1921.

# THE EMPEROR JONES

## 1921-1928

### 22

## THEATRE ARTS MAGAZINE

Theatre Arts Magazine, published monthly in New York City, issue for January, 1921 [Vol. 5, No. 1].

Collation: 8vo. [leaf measures 9½ x 6¼ inches]; pp. 88; pp. 29-59, contain play in eight scenes, "The Emperor Jones" by Eugene G. O'Neill.

Issued in buff wrappers. Front cover contains in brown, "Theatre Arts/Magazine/[line-cut of building]/Volume V —Number 1/January 1921."

*See illustration opposite.*

This is the first printing of the play. This is the text which was used — with many incidental editorial changes — for the edition published by Stewart Kidd Company No. 25.

The Boni and Liveright edition No. 23 contains a revised version which was prepared by the author. Dialogue and dialect vary in all three versions.

Errors for identification:

    P. 39, l. 30 — First word should be "Not."

    P. 47, l. 27 — Should be "fencing" instead of "forming."

    P. 58, l. 11 — Should be "gutturally" instead of "guttarally."

    P. 59, l. 10 — Should be "all" instead of "al."

### 23

FIRST EDITION

# THE EMPEROR JONES
# DIFF'RENT
# THE STRAW

The Emperor Jones / Diff'rent / The Straw / By / Eugene G. O'Neill / Boni & Liveright / Publishers New York / [1921]

*See facsimile p. 29.*

Collation: 12mo. [leaf measures 7⅜ x 5 inches]; pp. 2 blank +xii+290, consisting of; p. [i], Half-title, "The Emperor Jones / Diff'rent / The Straw"; p. [ii], contains, "Plays by / Eugene G. O'Neill / [single-line] / 1. Beyond the Horizon / 2. The Moon of the Caribbees / And Six other Plays of the Sea / 3. The Emperor Jones; Diff'rent; / The Straw / In Preparation / 4. Gold / 5. The Ole Devil" / [all of which is enclosed in single-line box]; p. [iii], Title-page as above; p. [iv], contains, "The Emperor Jones / Diff'rent / The Straw / [short line] / Copyright, 1921, by / Boni & Liveright, Inc. / [short line] / All rights reserved / [Permission clause for acting rights — the American Play Co. Inc., 33 West 42nd Street, New York City] / The Emperor Jones and Diff'rent were first produced / by the

# THE EMPEROR JONES
# DIFF'RENT
# THE STRAW

BY

EUGENE G. O'NEILL

BONI AND LIVERIGHT

PUBLISHERS                    NEW YORK

(No. 23)

*Title-page of the first edition*

Provincetown Players, 133 Macdougal Street, / New York City."; p. [v], Table of Contents; p. [vi], blank; p. [vii], Half-title, "The Straw"; p. [viii], blank; p. ix, List of Characters in "The Straw"; p. x, List of Acts and Scenes in "The Straw"; p. [xi], Half-Title, "Act I"; p. [xii], blank; pp. 1-142, Text of "The Straw"; pp. [143]-197, Text of "The Emperor Jones"; pp. [199]-285, Text of "Diff'rent"; pp. 286-290, blank.

Issued in buff boards lettered on front cover in black, "The Emperor Jones / Diff'rent [two small ornaments] / The Straw / Eugene G. O'Neill". Spine is light tan cloth lettered in black, "The / Emperor / Jones [small ornament] / Diff'rent / The / Straw / Eugene G. / O'Neill / Boni and / Liveright". All edges are cut, and end papers are plain. Issued in cream colored dust wrapper.

First published in April, 1921.
First printing consisted of 2200 copies.

"The Emperor Jones" first appeared in The Theatre Arts Magazine, January, 1921. See No. 22.

The first issue conforms in general format with Nos. 14 and 18, but the color, the board covers and cloth spine are uniform with later issues of "Beyond the Horizon." See No. 18. In other words, the boards are light buff and the spine is light tan. The second issue of this volume has very light buff, mottled boards and on the spine "Boni and / Liveright" is in script-style type. It has no "G." in name of author on front cover or spine.

*See illustration p. 65.*

The text of "The Emperor Jones" as it appeared in the Theatre Arts Magazine was thoroughly edited by the author for its use in this volume. Consequently, the variations in words and phrases between the two texts is thus explained. Furthermore, it will be noticed by comparing the text of the Theatre Arts Magazine and that in the separate edition published by Stewart Kidd Company, No. 25, that there is greater similarity. This fact led to the early conclusion that the Stewart Kidd edition was the first published. Such is not the case as may be seen by the dates of publication. It is true, however, that the Stewart Kidd edition was published — with minor editorial changes by Frank Shay — from the text of the Theatre Arts Magazine.

Errors for identification:

P. 30, l. 19 — Should be "sighs" instead of "signs."
P. 152, l. 30 — Should be "cows" instead of "cowers."
P. 156, l. 17 — Should be "any" instead of "ary."
P. 169, l. 23 — Should be "wouldn't" instead of "wouldn'."
P. 236, l. 18 — The word "like" should be inserted after "slip."

## 24

### ENGLISH EDITION

Plays: First Series / The Straw, The Emperor / Jones, and Diff'rent / By Eugene O'Neill / [Publisher's Device] / With an introduction by C. E. Bechhofer / Jonathan Cape / Eleven Gower Street, London / [1922]

Collation: Crown 8vo; pp. x+282.

Issued in bright blue cloth, no printing on front cover but with white title label pasted on spine. Issued in cream colored dust wrapper.

First published in May, 1922.

Contains same plays as American Edition No. 23 but has a four-page introduction by Bechhofer.

*Uniform with No. 15.*

## 25

# THE EMPEROR JONES

### FIRST SEPARATE EDITION

The Emperor Jones / By / Eugene O'Neill / Author of "Iles," "Bound East for Cardiff," etc. / First Performed by the Provincetown Players, November, 1920. / [Publisher's Device] / Cincinnati / Stewart Kidd Company / Publishers [1921]

Collation: 12mo. [leaf measures $7\frac{1}{2}$ x $5\frac{1}{16}$ inches]; pp. 56, consisting of; p. [1], Half-title, "Stewart Kidd Modern Plays /Edited by Frank Shay/The Emperor Jones"; p. [2], contains full-page advertisement for the Stewart Kidd Modern Play series; p. [3], Title-page as above; p. [4], contains, "Copyright, 1921 /Stewart Kidd Company/ [short line] /All rights reserved / Copyright in England" [all of which is enclosed in a single-line box] / [Permission clause for acting rights — American Play Company, Inc., 33 West 42nd Street, New York City]; p. [5], List of Characters; p. [6], blank; pp. 7-54, Text of "The Emperor Jones" in eight scenes; p. [55], full-page advertisement of Eugene O'Neill's Books already published by Boni & Liveright; p. [56], full-page advertisement for "European Theories of the Drama" by Barrett H. Clark.

Issued in white wrappers lettered on front cover in black, "The / Emperor / Jones / By / Eugene O'Neill / [decoration in olive green] /Steward Kidd /Modern Plays /Edited by/ Frank Shay". Also, on front cover at extreme right and left are three $\frac{1}{4}''$ olive green stripes $\frac{3}{16}''$ apart running from top to bottom. Back cover has advertisement for Stewart Kidd Dramatic Publications. Inside front cover has advertisement for "The Provincetown Plays" edited by George Cram Cook, and inside back cover has advertisement for "Fifty Contemporary One-Act Plays" edited by Frank Shay and Pierre Loving. All edges are cut.

First published in September, 1921.
First printing consisted of 2000 copies.

See note in regard to this text under No. 23.
Errors for identification:
      Title-page — Should be "Ile" instead of "Iles."
      P. 16, l. 28 — Should be "any" instead of "ary."
      P. 26, l. 28 — Should be "you" instead of "and."
      P. 27, l. 13 — The "i" is missing from "in."

## 26

### SEPARATE ENGLISH EDITION

The Emperor Jones / A Play by / Eugene O'Neill / [Publisher's Device] / Jonathan Cape Ltd / Thirty Bedford Square London / [1925]

Collation: Crown 8vo.; pp. viii+56.
Issued in green boards — some in wrappers — lettered on front cover in black, "The Emperor Jones/Eugene O'Neill". Spine has lettered in black, "The Emperor Jones * Eugene O'Neill". Issued in dust cover of same paper as that on the board cover.

First published in September, 1925.

Also contains the introduction by Bechhofer which first appeared in No. 24.

## 27

The/Emperor Jones/By/Eugene O'Neill/with
/Eight Illustrations/By/Alexander King/New
York — Boni & Liveright — 1928

Collation: 8vo. [leaf measures 10⅛ x 7½ inches]; pp. ii+
94, consisting of; pp. [i-ii], and [1], blank; p. [2], Certificate of issue with signature of author; p. [3], Half-title, "The
Emperor Jones"; p. [4], blank; p. [5], Title-page as above
printed in brown; p. [6], contains, "Copyright, 1928, by /
Boni & Liveright, Inc. / Printed in the United States of America"/[Permission clause for acting rights — author's agent];
p. [7], List of Characters; p. [8], blank; p. [9], List of
Scenes; p. [10], blank; p. [11], List of Illustrations; p. [12],
blank; p. [13], Half-title, "Scene One"; p. [14], blank; pp.
15-90, Text of "The Emperor Jones" in eight scenes; p. [91],
Colophon; pp. [92-94], blank. Contains eight illustrations in
color by Alexander King.

Issued in black, blue, red, green and gilt decorative boards,
with no printing on front cover. Spine is black vellum cloth,
lettered in gilt, "The Emperor Jones · Eugene O'Neill". Edges
are uncut and unopened. End papers are black-faced. Issued in
olive dust wrappers with black board slip-cover.

Published in July, 1928.
Edition limited to 775 copies of which 750 were for sale.

*Uniform with Nos. 32 and 33.*

# 28

# GOLD

Gold / A Play in Four Acts / By / Eugene G. O'Neill / [Publisher's Device] / Boni and Liveright / Publishers New York / [1921]

Collation: 12mo. [leaf measures 7½ x 5⅛ inches]; pp. viii+ 120, consisting of; p. [i], Half-title, "Gold"; p. [ii], contains, "Plays by / Eugene G. O'Neill / [single-line] / The Moon of the Caribbees and Six Other Plays of the Sea / Beyond the Horizon / The Straw / Gold" [all of which is contained in single-line box]; p. [iii], Title-page as above; p. [iv], Contains at bottom, "Gold / [short line] / Copyright, 1920, by / Boni & Liveright, Inc. / [short line] / Printed in the United States of America"; p. [v], List of Acts and Scenes; p. [vi], blank; p. [vii], Half-title "Act I"; p. [viii] List of Characters; pp. 1-120, Text of the four-act play.

Issued in green boards lettered on front cover in black, "Gold/Eugene G. O'Neill". Spine is olive green cloth lettered in black, "Gold/Eugene G./O'Neill/Boni &/Liveright." All edges are cut. End papers are plain. Issued with light yellow dust wrapper.

First published in September, 1921.
First printing consisted of 1200 copies.

It should be noted that the date of publication is one year later than the date of copyright.
This volume is uniform with No. 14 except for the color of binding.

Errors for identification:
P. 59, l. 1 — Should be "snivelin'" instead of "snivvelin'."
P. 65, l. 17 — In first act the word "fella" here is changed to "falla."
P. 83, l. 20 — Should be "I'll" instead of "I'l."

[ENGLISH EDITION]

*See No.* 19, *Beyond the Horizon.*

# THE HAIRY APE
# "ANNA CHRISTIE"
# THE FIRST MAN

## 1922-1930

## 29

### FIRST EDITION

The Hairy Ape / Anna Christie / The First Man / By / Eugene O'Neill / Boni and Liveright / Publishers New York / [1922]

Collation: 12mo. [leaf measures 7⅜ x 5 inches]; pp. xii+ 324, consisting of; p. [i], Half-title, "The Hairy Ape / Anna Christie / The First Man" / [Publisher's Device in lower right-hand corner]; p. [ii], contains, "Plays by / Eugene O'Neill / [single-line] / 1. Beyond the Horizon / 2. The Moon of the Caribbees / And Six other plays of the Sea / 3. The Emperor Jones; Diff'rent; / The Straw / 4. The Hairy Ape; Anna Christie; The First Man / In Preparation / 5. The Fountain" [all of which is enclosed in a single-line box]; p. [iii], Title-page as above; p. [iv], contains, "The Hairy Ape / Anna Christie / The First Man / [short line] / Copyright, 1922, by / Boni & Liveright, Inc. / [short line] / All rights reserved" / [short line] / [Permission clause for acting rights — American Play Company, Inc., 33 West 42nd Street, New York City.] / [Record of "first productions"]; p. [v], Table of Contents; p. [vi], blank; p. [vii], Half-title, "The Hairy Ape / A Comedy of Ancient and Modern Life / In Eight Scenes / By / Eugene O'Neill"; p. [viii], blank; p. [ix], List of Characters; p. [x], List of Scenes; p. [xi], Half-title, "Scene I"; p. [xii], blank; pp. 1-87, Text of "The Hairy Ape" in eight Scenes; pp. [89]-211, Text of "Anna Christie" in four acts; pp. [213]-322, Text of "The First Man" in four acts; pp. [323-324], blank.

Issued in buff boards, lettered on front cover in black, "The Hairy Ape / Anna Christie / The First Man / Eugene O'Neill." Spine is light tan cloth lettered in black, "The / Hairy Ape / Anna / Christie / The / First Man / Eugene / O'Neill / Boni and / Liveright". All edges are cut, and end papers are plain. Issued in cream colored dust wrapper.

First published in July, 1922.
First printing consisted of 2620 copies.

This volume is uniform with No. 14.
Errors for identification:
    P. 37, l. 16 — "To" is missing after first "gat."
    P. 104, l. 8 — Should be "engrossed" instead of "engrosesd."
    P. 140, l. 1 — "Half smiling" should be in italics.

## 30

ENGLISH EDITION

The Hairy Ape / and other Plays by / Eugene O'Neill / [Publisher's Device] / Jonathan Cape / Eleven Gower Street, London / [1923]

Collation: Crown 8vo.; pp. vii+311, each play having separate pagination.

Issued in bright blue cloth, no printing on front cover but with white title label pasted on spine. Issued in cream colored dust wrapper.

First published in June, 1923.

This volume contains the same plays and in the same order as the American first edition No. 29 "The Hairy Ape," "Anna Christie," and "The First Man."

*Uniform with No. 15.*

## 31

## ANNA CHRISTIE

FIRST SEPARATE EDITION

Anna Christie / A Play in Four Acts by / Eugene O'Neill / [Publisher's Device] / Jonathan Cape / Eleven Gower Street, London / [1923]

*See facsimile p. 39.*

Collation: Crown 8vo. [leaf measures 7½ x 5 inches]; pp. iv+122, consisting of; p. [i], Half-title, "Anna Christie"; p.

# Anna Christie

A Play in Four Acts *by*

## Eugene O'Neill

## Jonathan Cape

Eleven Gower Street, London

(No. 31)

*Title-page of the first separate edition*

[ii], contains, "By the same Author / Plays First Series / The Moon of the Caribbees and other Plays / The Hairy Ape and other Plays"; p. [iii], Title-page as above; p. [iv], contains, "First Published 1923 / All rights reserved"; p. [1], Half-title, "Anna Christie"; p. [2], contains, "Printed in Great Britain by Butler & Tanner, Frome and London"; p. 3, List of Characters; p. 4, List of Acts; pp. 5-122, Text of "Anna Christie," a play in four acts.

Issued in yellow boards — some in wrappers — lettered on front cover in black, "Anna Christie / Eugene O'Neill. Spine is lettered in black, "Anna / Christie / [ornament] / Eugene / O'Neill / Jonathan / Cape." Top edges are cut, others are uncut. End papers are plain. Issued in yellow dust wrapper of same paper as that on board covers.

First published in May, 1923.

## 32

# THE HAIRY APE

### SEPARATE AND ILLUSTRATED EDITION

The / Hairy Ape / By / Eugene O'Neill / with / Nine / Illustrations / By / Alexander King / New York — Horace Liveright — 1929

Collation: 8vo. [leaf measures 10 x 7½ inches]; pp. 116, consisting of; p. [1], blank; p. [2], Certificate of issue with signature of author; p. [3], Half-title, "The Hairy Ape"; p. [4], blank; p. [5], Title-page as above printed in brown; p. [6], contains "Copyright, 1922, by / Boni and Liveright, Inc. / Copyright, 1929, by / Horace Liveright, Inc. / [short line] / Printed in the U. S. A."; p. [7], List of Illustrations; p. [8],

blank; p. [9], List of Characters; p. [10], blank; p. [11],
List of Scenes; p. [12], blank; p. [13], Half-title, "Scene
One"; p. 14, blank; pp. 15-114, Text of "The Hairy Ape"
in eight scenes; p. [115], Colophon; p. [116], blank. Contains nine illustrations in color by Alexander King.

Issued in blue and red decorative boards, with no printing
on front cover. Spine is black vellum cloth, lettered in gilt,
"The Hairy Ape · Eugene O'Neill". Edges are uncut and unopened. End papers are black-faced. Issued in gray dust wrapper with black board slip-cover.

Published in April, 1929.
Edition limited to 775 copies of which 750 were for sale.

*Uniform with Nos. 27 and 33.*

# 33

## ANNA CHRISTIE

### ILLUSTRATED EDITION

"Anna / Christie" / By / Eugene O'Neill / with /
Twelve Illustrations / By / Alexander King / New
York — Horace Liveright — 1930

Collation: 8vo. [leaf measures 10⅛ x 7½ inches]; pp. 164,
consisting of; p. [1], blank; p. [2], Certificate of issue with
signature of author; p. [3], Half-title, '"Anna Christie"'; p.
[4], blank; p. [5] Title-page as above printed in sea-green;
p. [6], contains, "Copyright, 1922, by Boni & Liveright, Inc.
/ Copyright, 1930, by Horace Liveright, Inc. / Manufactured
in the U. S. A." / [Permission clause for acting rights — author's agent]; p. [7], List of Characters; p. [8], blank; p.
[9], List of Acts; p. [10], blank; p. [11], List of Illustra-

tions; p. [12], blank; p. [13], Half-title, "Act One"; p. [14], blank; pp. 15-161, Text of '"Anna Christie"' in four acts; pp. [162-164], blank. Contains twelve illustrations in color by Alexander King.

Issued in purple and red decorative boards with no printing on front cover. Spine is black vellum cloth, lettered in gilt, '"Anna Christie" · Eugene O'Neill'. Edges are uncut and unopened. End papers are black-faced. Issued in blue dust wrapper with black board slip-cover.

Published in November, 1930.
Edition limited to 775 copies of which 750 were for sale.

*Uniform with Nos. 27 and 32.*

Numbers 26-37 of this edition were bound in purple full levant with a facsimile of the author's signature stamped in gilt on the front cover and with "Anna / Christie / Eugene / O'Neill / Illustrated / By / Alexander / King" stamped in gilt on the spine. Tipped into each of the twelve volumes is a cellophane envelope which contains one of the original illustrations signed by the artist. These volumes were published in December, 1930.

# PROVINCETOWN PLAYBILL

## 1923-1925

## 34

A contribution, entitled, "Strindberg and Our Theatre" in the Provincetown Playbill — a program for the Provincetown Playhouse, New York City — issue No. 1 for the season of 1923-1924.

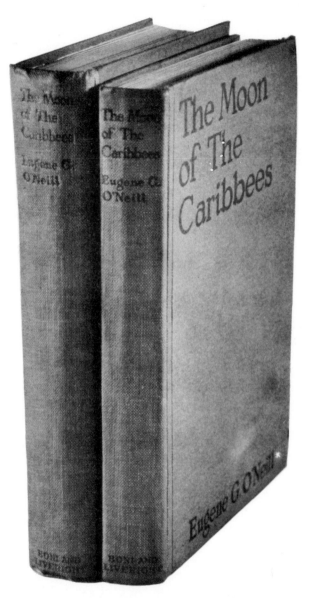

SECOND ISSUE            FIRST ISSUE

(No. 14)

*Showing variations in size*

## 35

Reproduction of four original sketches of sets for "Desire Under the Elms" in the Provincetown Playbill — issue No. 5 for the season of 1924-1925.

## 36

A contribution, entitled, "Are the Actors to Blame?" in the Provincetown Playbill — issue No. 1 for the season of 1925-1926.

# ALL GOD'S CHILLUN GOT WINGS

## 1924-1925

## 37

## THE AMERICAN MERCURY

The American Mercury, a magazine published monthly in New York City, issue for February, 1924 [Vol. 1, No. 2].

Collation: 8vo. [leaf measures 10 x 6⅛ inches]; pp. xvi+ 256; pp. 129-148, contain play in two acts, "All God's Chillun Got Wings" by Eugene O'Neill.

Issued in green wrappers. Front cover contains decorative border within which is "Vol. 1 February 1924 No. 2 / The / American / Mercury / A Monthly Review / Edited by H. L.

Mencken /& George Jean Nathan /[Monogram] / 50¢ $5.00 / For one Copy By the Year / Alfred A. Knopf / Publisher."

## 38

### FIRST EDITION

## ALL GOD'S CHILLUN GOT WINGS
## WELDED

All God's Chillun / Got Wings / and / Welded / By/Eugene O'Neill /[Publisher's Device] /Boni and Liveright / Publisher :: :: New York / [1924]

Collation: 12mo. [leaf measures 7½ x 5⅛ inches]; pp. 172, consisting of; p. [1], Half-title, "All God's Chillun / Got Wings / Welded"; p. [2], contains, "Books by / Eugene O'Neill / [single-line] / Beyond the Horizon / The Moon of the Caribbees and Six Other/Plays of the Sea/The Emperor Jones; Diff'rent; The Straw/The Hairy Ape; Anna Christie; The First/Man/All God's Chillun Got Wings; Welded"/ [all of which is enclosed in a single-line box]; p. [3], Title-page as above; p. [4], contains, "Copyright, 1924, by / Boni & Liveright, Inc./[short line]/Printed in the United States of America" / [Permission clause for acting rights — author's agent]; p. [5], Table of Contents; p. [6], blank; p. [7], Half-title, "All God's Chillun/Got Wings"; p. [8], blank; p. [9], List of Characters; p. [10], blank; p. [11], List of Acts and Scenes; p. [12], blank; p. [13], Half-title, "Act I"; p. [14], blank; pp. 15-[80], Text of "All Gods Chillun Got Wings" in two acts; p. [81]-170, Text of "Welded" in three acts; pp. [171-172], blank.

Issued in buff boards, lettered on front cover in black. "All God's Chillun / Got Wings and / Welded / Eugene O'Neill." Spine is light tan cloth, lettered in black, "All God's / Chillun / Got Wings / and / Welded / [small solid triangle inverted] / Eugene / O'Neill / [Blind stamp of publisher's device] / Boni & / Liveright". Top and bottom edges are cut, side edges are uncut. End papers are plain and there is an extra leaf, front and back. Issued in light brown dust wrapper.

First published in April, 1924.
First printing consisted of 3200 copies.

"All God's Chillun Got Wings" first appeared in The American Mercury, February, 1924. See No. 37.
This volume is uniform with No. 14.
There are a few minor variations in this text from the one given in "The American Mercury," such as "Sissy" for "Cissy" on p. 18, l. 5, — "for" for "fer" on p. 27, l. 13 — "Bonbon for "Bon Bon" on p. 31, l. 14, and "to" for "too" on p. 44, l. 9.

# 39

### ENGLISH EDITION

All God's Chillun Got Wings / Desire Under the Elms / and Welded / by / Eugene O'Neill / [Publisher's Device] / Jonathan Cape Ltd. / Thirty Bedford Square, London / [1925]

Collation: Crown 8vo.; pp. vi+282, each play having separate pagination.

Issued in bright blue cloth, no printing on front cover, but with white title label pasted on spine. Issued in cream colored dust wrapper.

First published·in October, 1925.

The first printing of "Desire Under the Elms" appeared in No. 44. Only the two plays "All God's Chillun Got Wings" and "Welded" were published together in American first edition No. 38.

*Uniform with No. 15.*

# GREENWICH PLAYBILL

## 1924-1925

### 40

Reproduction of an original sketch for a setting in "Desire Under the Elms," entitled, "The Cabot Homestead" in the Greenwich Playbill — a program for the Greenwich Village Theatre, New York City — issue No. 2 for the season of 1924-1925.

### 41

A "note" in the program for "The Fountain" which is Greenwich Playbill, issue No. 3 for the season of 1925-1926.

# COLLECTED PLAYS

## TWO VOLUMES

### 42

## [VOLUME I]

The / Complete Works / of / Eugene O'Neill / Volume One / [Publisher's Device in green] / New York / Boni & Liveright / 1924 [1925]

[All of which is contained in a green line box with decorative top and bottom.]

Collation: 8vo. [leaf measures 8⅞ x 5⅞ inches]; pp. vi+ 504, consisting of; p. [i], Half-title, "The / Complete Works / of / Eugene O'Neill / [short line] / Volume One"; p. [ii], Certificate of issue with signature of author; p. [iii], Title-page as above; p. [iv], contains, "The / Complete Works / of / Eugene O'Neill / [short line] / Copyrighted, 1924, by / Boni & Liveright, Inc. / [short line] / Volume I." [followed by a record of the separate copyrights for each play in the volume]; p. [v], Table of Contents; p. [vi], blank; p. [1], Half-title, ' "Anna Christie" / A Play in Four Acts / (1920)'; p. [2], blank; p. [3], List of Characters; p. [4], List of Acts; pp. 5-502, Text of —

> "Anna Christie"
> Beyond the Horizon
> "The First Man"
> Diff'rent
> Gold
> The Moon of the Caribbees

Bound East for Cardiff
The Long Voyage Home
In the Zone
Ile;
pp. [503-504], blank.

Issued in gray boards, with gilt facsimile of author's signature on front cover. Spine is blue cloth, lettered in gilt, "Collected / Plays / of / Eugene / O'Neill / [all of which is enclosed in gilt border similar in design to that on title-page] / [Gilt star] / [Blind stamp of publisher's device] / Boni and / Liveright" / [Border in gilt of same decoration as above]. Edges are uncut and unopened. End papers are plain. Issued in gray board slip-cover containing this volume and volume II.

*See also No. 43 footnote.*

Published in January, 1925.
Edition limited to 1200 numbered sets with Volume II.

## 43

### [Volume II]

The / Complete Works / of / Eugene O'Neill / Volume Two / [Publisher's Device in green] / New York / Boni & Liveright / 1924 [1925]

[All of which is enclosed by a green border with decorative top and bottom.]

Collation: 8vo. [leaf measures 8⅞ x 5⅞ inches]; pp. vi+ 458, consisting of; p. [i], Half-title, "The / Complete Works / of / Eugene O'Neill / [short line] / Volume Two"; p. [ii], blank; p. [iii], Title-page as above; p. [iv], contains, "The / Complete Works / of / Eugene O'Neill / [short line] / Copyrighted, 1924, by/Boni & Liveright, Inc./[short line]/Volume II." / [followed by a record of the separate copyrights for each play in the volume]; p. [v], Table of Contents; p. [vi], blank; p. [1], Half-title, "The Emperor Jones/(1920)"; p. [2], blank; p. [3], List of Characters; p. [4], List of Scenes; pp. 5-457, Text of —

> The Emperor Jones
> "The Hairy Ape"
> All God's Chillun Got Wings
> Desire Under the Elms
> Welded
> The Straw
> The Rope
> The Dreamy Kid
> Where the Cross is Made
> Before Breakfast;

p. [458], blank.

Issued uniform with Volume I described previously except that spine has two gilt stars.

This volume [II] contains the first printing of "Desire Under the Elms," a play in three parts. It was published separately in April, 1925, No. 44.

Published in January, 1925.

Edition limited to 1200 numbered sets with Volume I.

Although dated on the title-page, 1924, these volumes were not published until 1925 as shown above.

## 44

## DESIRE UNDER THE ELMS

### FIRST SEPARATE EDITION

Provincetown-Greenwich Plays / Desire Under /
The Elms / Eugene O'Neill / [Publisher's Device]
/ New York / Boni & Liveright / 1925

[All of which is enclosed in double-line box with additional double-line running width of box under first line above.]

Collation: 12mo. [leaf measures $7\frac{7}{16}$ x $5\frac{1}{8}$ inches]; pp. 168
[with pp. [1] and [2] missing but with extra leaf at end,
making total given here] consisting of; p. [3], Half-title,
"Provincetown-Greenwich Plays / [single-line] / Desire Under
the Elms"; p. [4], blank; p. [5], Title-page as above; p. [6],
contains, "Copyright, 1924, by Boni & Liveright, Inc. / Copyright, 1925, by Boni & Liveright, Inc." / [Permission clause for
acting rights — author's agent]; p. [7], Half-title, "Desire
Under the Elms / A Play in Three Parts"; p. [8], blank; p.
[9], List of Characters; p. [10], blank; pp. 11-12, Story of
the action and setting; pp. 13-166, Text of "Desire Under the
Elms," a play in three parts; pp. [167-168], blank.

Issued in black cloth, decorated on front cover with red win-
dow through which may be seen white silhouette of ship and
pier under which is lettered "Provincetown / - Greenwich /
Plays", all of which being stamped into cover. Spine has lettered in red, "Provincetown / -Greenwich / Plays / [double-
line] / Desire / Under the / Elms / [small decoration] / O'Neill
/ Boni & / Liveright." Top edges are cut and stained red, other

edges are uncut and plain. End papers are plain. Issued with light-yellow dust wrapper.

First published in April, 1925.
First printing consisted of 2000 copies.

This play was first published in the Limited Edition [Volume 2] of the Collected Plays of Eugene O'Neill No. 43.
Errors for identification:
    P. 87, l. 4 — Bracket at end of line missing.
    P. 96, l. 4 — Should read "away" instead of "awaw."

[ENGLISH EDITION]

*See No.* 40.


# THE WORKS OF EUGENE O'NEILL

### FOUR VOLUMES

## 45

### [VOLUME I]

## "ANNA CHRISTIE"

## ALL GOD'S CHILLUN GOT WINGS

## DIFF'RENT

Eugene O'Neill / [Green line] / Plays / "Anna Christie" / All God's Chillun Got Wings / Diff'-rent / [Green line] / [Publisher's Device in green] / [Green line] / New York / Boni & Liveright / 1925

# EUGENE O'NEILL

## *Plays*

### "ANNA CHRISTIE"
### ALL GOD'S CHILLUN GOT WINGS
### DIFF'RENT

### *NEW YORK*
### BONI & LIVERIGHT
### 1 9 2 5

(No. 44)

*Title-page of first volume of trade edition of collected plays*

[All of which is contained in green line box with decorative top and bottom.]

*See facsimile p. 52.*

Collation: 8vo. [leaf measures $8\frac{3}{16}$ x $5\frac{7}{16}$ inches]; pp. 256, consisting of; p. [1], Half-title, "Eugene O'Neill / [single-line] / "Anna Christie" / All God's Chillun Got Wings / Diff'rent"; p. [2], Contains, "Plays of / Eugene O'Neill / [single line] / Uniform with this edition / Beyond the Horizon / The Straw / Before Breakfast / In one volume / [short line] / The Emperor Jones / Gold / The First Man, and / The Dreamy Kid / In one volume / [short line] / Desire Under the Elms / The Hairy Ape, and / Welded / In one volume" / [All of which is contained in single-line box]; p. [3], Title-page as above; p. [4], Contains, "Plays of Eugene O'Neill / Copyright, 1925, by / Boni & Liveright, Inc. / [short line] / Printed in the United States of America" / [short line] / [separate copyrights for plays in this volume] / [Permission Clause for acting rights — author's agent]; p. [5], Table of Contents; p. [6], blank; p. [7], Half-title, '"Anna Christie" / A play in Four Acts / (1920)'; p. [8], blank; p. [9], List of Acts; p. [10], List of Characters; p. [11], Half-title, '"Anna Christie" / Act One"'; p. [12], blank; pp. 13-254, Text of the three plays; pp. [255-256], blank.

Issued in sea-green vellum cloth, with gilt facsimile signature of the author, and blue single-line scroll border on front cover. Spine has lettered in gilt, "Eugene / O'Neill / [Decoration] / Anna / Christie / All God's / Chillun / Got Wings / Diff'-rent / [Blind stamp of publisher's device] / Boni and / Liveright" / [with decorative border line in gilt at top and bottom of spine]. Top edges are cut and stained black, others are uncut and plain. End papers are colored in buff and green, and have illustration of silhouetted tramp-steamer against rising full moon at left and with high waves and lone gull at right. Issued in blue-green dust wrapper.

First published in July, 1925.
First printing consisted of 2000 copies.

*See note under No. 48.*


# 46

## [VOLUME II]

## BEYOND THE HORIZON

## THE STRAW

## BEFORE BREAKFAST

Uniform with volume one in binding, dust wrapper, size, and number of pages [256]. Front matter has same sequence except that there is an extra leaf not appearing in volume one on p. [9] of which is half-title, "To Agnes," a dedication preceding, "Beyond the Horizon," which is the first play in this volume. Also, names of plays are here substituted in the order shown above.

First published in July, 1925.
First printing consisted of 1200 copies.

*See note under No. 48.*

## 47

### [VOLUME III]

# DESIRE UNDER THE ELMS
# "THE HAIRY APE"
# WELDED

Uniform with volume one in binding, dust wrapper, and size. This volume has 240 pages and front matter has an extra leaf not appearing in volume one on p. [11] on which is the prose description of the action and setting for "Desire Under the Elms" which is the first play in this volume. Also, names of plays are here substituted in the order shown above.

First published in July, 1925.
First printing consisted of 2000 copies.

*See note under No. 48.*

## 48

### [VOLUME IV]

# THE EMPEROR JONES
# GOLD
# "THE FIRST MAN"
# THE DREAMY KID

Uniform with volume one in binding, dust wrapper, size, and number of pages [256]. Front matter has same sequence except that there is one less leaf here inasmuch as there is no half-title preceding the first scene of "The Emperor Jones" which is the first play in this volume. Also, names of plays are here substituted in the order shown above.

First published in July, 1925.
First printing consisted of 2000 copies.

This trade edition of the collected plays differs from the limited edition Nos. 42 and 43 inasmuch as it does not contain "The Moon of the Caribbees and Six Other Plays of the Sea" which were originally published in 1919 No. 14. These plays were included in a later volume which is uniform with those described here, No. 53.

The plays, "Beyond the Horizon," "Welded," "Gold" and "The Straw" as they appear here have been shortened somewhat since their original publication, Nos. 18, 38, 28 and 23, respectively. Also, minor editorial changes have been made and previous errors corrected in all of the plays.

## 49

## BOSTON EVENING TRANSCRIPT

"Playwright and Critic: The Record of a Stimulating Correspondence" [Eugene O'Neill to George Jean Nathan], a series of letters included in that article by Isaac Goldberg on p. 8 [entire page] of Part III of the Boston Evening Transcript, a newspaper published week-days in Boston, Massachusetts, issue for October 31, 1925.

This correspondence was reprinted in "The Theatre of George Jean Nathan" by Isaac Goldberg, New York, 1927.

SECOND ISSUE    (No. 18)    FIRST ISSUE

*Showing variations in type face and different spine cloths and cover boards*

# NEW YORK EVENING POST
## 1926-1929

### 50

A letter to the press, entitled "Eugene O'Neill Writes about his Latest Play" ["The Great God Brown"] on p. 6 of the Drama Section of the New York Evening Post, a newspaper published weekdays in New York City, issue of February 13, 1926.

This was also printed under various titles in other New York papers the following day.

### 51

A contribution, entitled, "O'Neill Talks about 'Beyond the Horizon'" on p. 6 of the Drama Section of the New York Evening Post, issue for November 27, 1926.

### 52

Reproductions of two original sketches of settings in "Dynamo" on p. 4M of the New York Evening Post, issue for February 9, 1929.

*See also No. 70.*

# THE GREAT GOD BROWN
# THE FOUNTAIN

## 53

### FIRST EDITION

[Uniform with four volumes of collected plays — trade edition published in 1925, No. 45.]

Eugene O'Neill / [Green line] / The Great God Brown / The Fountain / The Moon of the Caribbees / and Other Plays / [Green line] / [Publisher's Device in green] / [green line] / New York / Boni & Liveright / 1926

[All of which is contained in green line box with decorative top and bottom.]

Collation: 8vo. [leaf measures $8\frac{1}{16}$ x $5\frac{7}{16}$ inches]; pp. 384, consisting of; p. [1], Half-title, "Eugene O'Neill / [single-line] / The Great God Brown / The Fountain / The Moon of the Caribbees / and Other Plays"; p. [2], Contains, "Plays of / Eugene O'Neill / [single line] / Uniform with this edition / The Emperor Jones / Gold / The First Man / The Dreamy Kid / In one volume / [short line] / Beyond the Horizon / The Straw / Before Breakfast / In one volume / [short line] / Anna Christie / All God's Chillun Got Wings / and Diff'rent / In one volume / [short line] / Desire Under the Elms / The Hairy Ape, and / Welded / In one volume" [all of which is contained in single-line box]; p. [3], Title-page as above; p. [4], contains, "Plays of Eugene O'Neill / Copyright, 1926, by / Boni & Liveright, Inc. / [short line] / Printed in the United States of America / [short line] / The Moon of the Caribbees, copyright, 1919, 1923, by / Boni & Liveright, Inc." / [Permission Clause for acting rights — author's agent.]; p. [5], Table of Contents; p. [6], blank; p. [7], Half-title, "The Great God Brown/(1920)"; p. [8], blank; p. [9], List of Characters; p. [10], List of Acts and Scenes; pp. 11-98, Text of "The Great God Brown" a play in four acts with prologue and epilogue; pp. [99]-192, Text of "The Fountain," a play in three parts; pp. [193]-383, Text of one-act plays, "The Moon of the Caribbees," "Bound East for Cardiff", "The Long Voyage Home", "In the Zone," "Ile," "Where the Cross is Made," and "The Rope"; p. [384], blank.

Issued in binding uniform with previous volumes in the trade edition of collected works No. 45. The dust wrapper, however, is different in design although uniform in color.

First published in March, 1926.
First printing consisted of 5000 copies.

Error for identification:
    P. 61, 1. 1 — Should be "Sköal" instead of "Shöal." Author has used former on p. 263, 1. 27.

# 54

ENGLISH EDITION

The Great God Brown / including The Fountain, The / Dreamy Kid and Before Breakfast / by / Eugene O'Neill / [Publisher's Device] / Jonathan Cape Ltd / Thirty Bedford Square London / [1926]

Collation: Crown 8vo.; pp. vi+280, each play having separate pagination.

Issued in bright blue cloth, no printing on front cover but with white title label pasted on spine. Issued in cream colored dust wrapper.

First published in September, 1926.

The two plays, "The Dreamy Kid" and "Before Breakfast" have been substituted for the one-act sea plays, "The Moon of the Caribbees," et cetera, which were included in the American Edition No. 53.

*Uniform with No. 15.*

## 55

# THE GREAT GOD BROWN

### FIRST SEPARATE EDITION

The Great God Brown / A Play in Four Acts by / Eugene O'Neill / [Publisher's Device] / Jonathan Cape / Thirty Bedford Square London / [1926]

Collation: Crown 8vo. [leaf measures $7\frac{7}{16}$ x 5 inches]; pp. iv+112 [with extra leaf front and back], consisting of; p. [i], Half-title, "The Great God Brown"; p. [ii], contains, "By the Same Author / The Emperor Jones / The Moon of the Caribbees / The Hairy Ape / Anna Christie / Beyond the Horizon / All God's Chillun ,Got Wings"; p. [iii], Title-page as above; p. [iv], contains, "First Published in MCMXXVI / Made & Printed in Great Britain / By Butler & Tanner Ltd / Frome and / London" / [small decoration]; p. [1], Half-title, "The Great God Brown"; p. [2], blank; p. [3], List of Characters; p. [4], blank; pp. 5-6, List of Acts and Scenes;

pp. 7-112, Text of "The Great God Brown", a play in four
acts, a prologue and an epilogue.

Issued in light blue wrappers, lettered on front cover in dark
blue, "The / Great God Brown / A Play in Four Acts By /
Eugene O'Neill / [Publisher's Device]" surrounded by decorative border at outside. Spine is lettered in dark blue, "The/
Great / God / Brown / Eugene / O'Neill / Jonathan / Cape"
with line of border at top and bottom of spine. Inside flap of
front cover has comments on O'Neill. Back cover has full-page
advertisement of other plays by O'Neill which have been published by Jonathan Cape. All edges are cut and end papers are
plain.

First published in July, 1926.

# EUGENE O'NEILL

## 1926-1929

## 56

### FIRST EDITION

Eugene O'Neill / By / Barrett H. Clark / Robert
M. McBride & Company / New York [six dotted
squares] 1926

Collation: 12mo.; pp. vi+114, and a photograph of O'Neill.

Issued in dark blue basket cloth with blind stamp of publisher's device on front cover. Spine is lettered in gilt "Modern / American / Writers / [decorative border line] / Eugene
/ O'Neill / [small ornament] / Clark / [decorative border line]
/ McBride" / [with decorative border line above and below all
of that]. Top edges cut, others are uncut. End papers are plain.
Issued in cream colored dust wrapper.

First published in August, 1926.

Contains several letters from O'Neill, excerpts from correspondence, and the entire poem, "It's Great When You Get In" which originally appeared on September 28, 1912, on editorial page of the New London Telegraph [See No. 2].

## 57

### REVISED EDITION

Eugene O'Neill / The Man and His Plays / By / Barrett H. Clark / [Publisher's Device] / New York / Robert M. McBride & Company / 1929

Collation: 12mo.; pp. xiv+214.

Issued in light blue buckram, lettered in gilt on front cover, "Eugene O'Neill / The Man and his Plays / [short double line] / Barrett H. Clark". Spine is lettered in gilt, "Eugene / O'Neill / [short double line] / Clark / McBride". Top edges are smooth and stained blue, other edges are uncut. End papers are plain. Issued in gray dust wrapper.

First published in April, 1929.

Contains some correspondence of O'Neill's not in previous edition No. 56.

## MARCO MILLIONS

## 58

### FIRST EDITION

[Uniform with four volumes of collected plays — trade edition published in 1925, No. 45.]

Eugene O'Neill / [Green line] / A Play / Marco Millions / [Green line] / [Publisher's Device in green] / [Green line] / New York / Boni & Liveright / 1927

[All of which is contained in green line box with decorative top and bottom.]

Collation: 8vo. [leaf measures 8⅛ x 5$\frac{7}{16}$ inches]; pp. 184, consisting of; p. [1], Half-title, "Marco Millions"; p. [2], blank; p. [3], Title-page as above; p. [4], Contains, "Copyright, 1927, by / Boni & Liveright, Inc. / [short line] / Printed in the United States of America" / [Permission clause for acting rights — author's agent.]; p. v, Forword; p. [6], blank; pp. vii and [8], List of Characters; p. ix, List of Acts and Scenes; p. [10], blank; p. [11], Half-title, "Prologue"; p. [12], blank; pp. 13-183, Text of "Marco Millions", a play in three acts, a prologue and an epilogue; p. [184], blank.

Issued in binding uniform with previous volumes in the trade edition of collected works No. 45. The dust wrapper is different in design although similar in color.

First published in April, 1927.
First printing consisted of 7500 copies.

This is the first long play to be published prior to its presentation on any stage.

The unusual pagination of the front matter should be noted.

Errors for identification:

    P. 90, l. 10 — Should be "His is" instead of "He is."

    P. 161, l. 2 — The word "is" should be indented to conform with rest of paragraph.

## 59

ENGLISH EDITION

Marco Millions / A Play / by / Eugene O'Neill / [Publisher's Device] / Jonathan Cape Ltd / Thirty Bedford Square London / [1927]

Collation: Crown 8vo.; pp. 160.

Issued in bright blue cloth, no printing on front cover but with white title label pasted on spine. Issued in cream colored dust wrapper.

First published in October, 1927.

This contains the same text and foreword as the American Edition No. 58.

*Uniform with No. 15.*

## 60

LIMITED EDITION

Marco / Millions / A Play by / Eugene O'Neill / [small rectangular illustration — $2\frac{1}{4}$ x $1\frac{5}{16}''$ — in orange flanked on either side by two horizontal lines $1\frac{1}{2}''$ apart] / New York / Boni and Liveright / 1927

[All of which surrounded by decorative border in orange and black.]

Collation: 8vo. [leaf measures $8\frac{7}{8}$ x $5\frac{3}{4}$ inches]; pp. 184, consisting of; p. [1], Half-title, "Marco Millions"; p. [2], Certificate of issue with Signature of author; p. [3], Title-

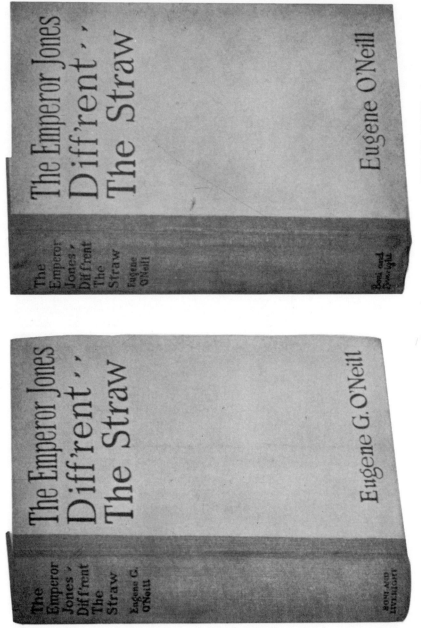

FIRST ISSUE  (No. 23)  SECOND ISSUE

*Showing variations in type face — different spine cloths and cover boards*

page as above; p. [4], Contains, "Copyright, 1927, by / Boni & Liveright, Inc. / [short line] / Printed in the United States of America" / [Permission clause for acting rights — author's agent.]; p. v, Foreword; p. [6], blank; pp. vii, and viii, List of Characters; p. ix, List of Acts and Scenes; p. [10], blank; p. [11], Half-title, "Prologue"; p. [12], blank; pp. 13-183, Text of "Marco Millions," a play in three acts, a prologue and an epilogue; p. [184], blank.

Issued in brown and gilt decorative boards, no printing on front cover. Spine is white parchment on which is pasted a brown title label containing, "Marco / Millions / A  Play / by / Eugene / O'Neill." Edges are uncut and unopened. End papers are plain. Issued in multi-colored board slip-cover.

Published in May, 1927.
Edition limited to 450 numbered copies of which 440 were for sale.

This volume was printed from the same plates as the trade edition and contains the errors and unusual pagination of that volume, No. 59. The front matter varies only insofar as p. [2] instead of being blank now contains the Certificate of issue and this title-page is more elaborate.

# 61

# A HISTORY OF THE AMERICAN
# DRAMA
## [Volume II]

A History of / The American Drama / From the Civil War to the Present Day / By / Arthur Hobson Quinn / Author of "A History of the American Drama from / the Beginning to the Civil War" /

Illustrated / [short line] / Volume II / From William Vaughn Moody / To the Present Day / [short line] / [Publisher's Device] / Harper & Brothers Publishers / New York and London / 1927

Collation: 8vo.; pp. xiv+362.
Issued in red cloth with gilt stamping on cover and spine. Top edges are cut, others are uncut. End papers are plain.

First published in October, 1927.

Contains correspondence from O'Neill. Some of which has been published elsewhere and is so identified.

## LAZARUS LAUGHED

## 62

## THE AMERICAN CARAVAN

### ACT I

The American / Caravan / [with border line above and below] / A Yearbook / of American Literature / Edited by / Van Wyck Brooks Lewis Mumford / Alfred Kreymborg Paul Rosenfeld / [two small squares] / New York / The Macaulay Company / [1927]

Collation: 8vo. [leaf measures 9¼ x 6¼ inches]; pp. xviii+ 846, consisting of; p. [i], Half-title, "The American / Caravan" / [with border line above and below as on Title-page]; p. [ii], blank; p. [iii], Title-page as above; p. [iv], contains, "Copyright, 1927, by / The Macaulay Company / Printed in the United States of America by / J. J. Little and Ives Company, New York"; p. [v], Dedication, "The First American Caravan / is inscribed by the Editors / to a Teacher, / Alfred Stieglitz"; p. [vi], blank; p. [vii] Poem by Stieglitz; p. [viii], blank; pp. ix-x, Foreword by editors; pp. xi-xiii, Table of Contents; p. [xiv], blank; pp. xv and xvi, Index of Authors; p. [xvii], Half-title, "The American Caravan"; p. [xviii], blank; pp. 1-806, Texts of the various contributions; pp. 807-833, Text of Act One of "Lazarus Laughed" by Eugene O'Neill with full list of characters, acts and scenes for the entire play in addition; p. [834], blank; pp. 835-843, Notes on Contributors; pp. [844-846], blank.

Issued in green cloth lettered in gilt on front cover, "The / American / Caravan" / [four lines of diminishing length below and one line and three-loop scroll above]. Spine contains same inscription and decoration [with three lines below] at top as appears on front cover, at bottom is single line and "Macaulay". Top edges are cut and stained light green, other edges are uncut. End papers are colored — light green and gray — with modernistic decoration. Issued with orange dust wrapper.

First published in September, 1927.
First printing consisted of 25,000 copies.

The author has explained this printing of the first act as being his response to a personal request from the editors for a contribution from him.

The text as given here differs substantially from that appearing in the published version of the entire play. *See No. 63.* As such it is of unique interest.

Error for identification:
In the text O'Neill's contribution.
P. 808, l. 5 from bottom — the last word in the line "are" should be in italics.

*See No. 63 for discussion of changes in text.*

*are masked in accordance with the following scheme: There are seven periods of life shown: Boyhood (or Girlhood), Youth, Young Manhood (or Womanhood), Manhood (or Womanhood), Middle Age, Maturity and Old Age—and each of these periods is represented by seven masks portraying general types of character as follows: 1. The Simple, Humble Type; 2. The Happy, Loving Type; 3. The Self-Tortured, Sensitive Type; 4. The Proud, Defiant Type; 5. The Servile, Envious Type; 6. The Revengeful, Cruel Type; 7. The Sorrowful, Resigned Type. Thus in each crowd (this includes the* SEVEN GUESTS *who are composed of one male of each Period and Type as Period One, Type One: Period Two, Type Two: and so on up to Period Seven, Type Seven; and also includes the* CHORUS OF SEVEN WOMEN *who are the female counterparts of the* SEVEN GUESTS *but whose masks mark them distinctively as the* CHORUS *in that they are double the life-size of all the others) there are forty-nine different combinations of Period and Type. Each Type has a distinct predominant color for its costumes which vary in kind according to its Period.*

*On a raised platform at the middle of the one table placed lengthwise at center sits* LAZARUS, *his head haloed and his body illumined by a soft radiance as of tiny phosphorescent flames caressing his flesh, now cleansed of the sorrow of death.*

*In appearance* LAZARUS *is tall, large-boned and powerful, about fifty years of age, with a mass of gray-black hair and a heavy beard. His face is dark-complected, ruddy and brown, the color of rich earth upturned by the plough, calm but furrowed deep with the marks of former suffering endured with a grim fortitude that had never softened into resignation. His forehead is broad and noble, his eyes black and deep-set. Just now he is staring straight before him as if his vision were still fixed beyond life.* LAZARUS *wears no mask. Kneeling beside him with bowed heads are his wife,* MIRIAM, *his sisters,* MARTHA *and* MARY, *and his* FATHER *and* MOTHER. MIRIAM *is a slender, delicate woman of thirty-six, dressed in deep black, who holds one of his hands in both of hers, and keeps her lips pressed to it. Her*

(No. 62)

*Specimen page from the first act of "Lazarus Laughed," first appearing in "The American Caravan"*

*by seven different masks of general types of character as
follows: The Simple, Ignorant; the Happy, Eager; the Self-
Tortured, Introspective; the Proud, Self-Reliant; the
Servile, Hypocritical; the Revengeful, Cruel; the Sorrowful,
Resigned. Thus in each crowd (this includes among the
men the Seven Guests who are composed of one male of
each period-type as period one—type one, period two—
type two, and so on up to period seven—type seven) there
are forty-nine different combinations of period and type.
Each type has a distinct predominant color for its costumes which varies in kind according to its period. The
masks of the Chorus of Old Men are double the size of
the others. They are all seven in the Sorrowful, Resigned
type of Old Age.]*

*On a raised platform at the middle of the one table placed
lengthwise at center sits* LAZARUS, *his head haloed and his
body illumined by a soft radiance as of tiny phosphorescent
flames.*

LAZARUS, *freed now from the fear of death, wears no
mask.*

*In appearance* LAZARUS *is tall and powerful, about fifty
years of age, with a mass of gray-black hair and a heavy
beard. His face recalls that of a statue of a divinity of
Ancient Greece in its general structure and particularly in
its quality of detached serenity. It is dark-complected,
ruddy and brown, the color of rich earth upturned by the
plow, calm but furrowed deep with the marks of former
suffering endured with a grim fortitude that had never
softened into resignation. His forehead is broad and
noble, his eyes black and deep-set. Just now he is staring*

*Specimen page from first edition of complete play*

# 63

[Uniform with four volumes of collected plays — trade edition published in 1925, No. 45.]

## Eugene O'Neill/[Green line]/Lazarus Laughed /(1925-26)/A Play For An Imaginative Theatre/[Green line]/[Publisher's Device in green] /[Green line]/New York/Boni & Liveright/ 1927

[All of which is contained in green line box with decorative top and bottom.]

Collation: 8vo. [leaf measures $8\frac{3}{16}$ x 5½ inches]; pp. ii+182, consisting of; pp. [i-ii], blank; p. [1], Half-title, "Lazarus Laughed"; p. [2], blank; p. [3], Title-page as above; p. [4], contains, "Copyright, 1927, by / Boni & Liveright, Inc. / [short line] / Printed in the United States of America" / [Permission clause for acting rights — author's agent.]; p. [5], List of Acts and Scenes, p. [6], blank; p. [7], List of Characters; p. [8], blank; p. [9], Half-title, "Act One"; p. [10], blank; pp. 11-179, Text of "Lazarus Laughed", a play in four acts; pp. [180-182], blank.

Issued in binding uniform with previous volumes in the trade edition of collected works, No. 45. The dust wrapper, however, is different in design although uniform in color.

First published on November 12, 1927.
First printing consisted of 7500 copies.

This is the first publication of the last three acts. Act I together with lists of characters, acts and scenes was published in "The

American Caravan." *See No.* 62. However, the author made numerous and very substantial changes in the text of act one between the time of its appearance in "The American Caravan" and in this volume. *See facsimiles pp.* 68 *and* 69. It is only one example of the comprehensive revising which the author makes on all manuscripts during the process of publication.

Errors for identification:

> P. [5], List of Acts and Scenes, Act I, Scene 4, — Should be "Dawn after same night." The American Caravan has "Dawn of the same day" but that is also incorrect.
>
> P. 148, l. 4 — Should be "lie" instead of "like."

## [ENGLISH EDITION]

*See No.* 72.

This was published in 1929 together with "Dynamo" and inasmuch as it is of considerable importance to the latter play, the collation has been given there.

# 64

## LIMITED EDITION

## Lazarus Laughed / By Eugene O'Neill / New York * Boni & Liveright * 1927

Collation: 8vo. [leaf measures 8⅞ x 5¾ inches]; pp. 182, consisting of; p. [1], Half-title, "Lazarus Laughed"; p. [2], Certificate of Issue with signature of author; p. [3], Title-page as above printed in light purple; p. [4], contains, "Copyright, 1927, by / Boni & Liveright, Inc. / [short line] / Printed in the United States of America" / [Permission clause for acting rights — author's agent.]; p. [5], List of Characters; p. [6], blank; p. [7], List of Acts and Scenes; p. [8], blank; p. [9], Half-title, "Act One"; p. [10], blank; pp. 11-179, Text of "Lazarus Laughed," a play in four acts; pp. [180-182], blank.

Issued in black boards with multicolored decorations, no printing on front cover. Spine is white parchment on which is pasted a light purple title label containing, "Lazarus / Laughed / [short line] / Eugene / O'Neill" / [with border line above and below]. Edges are uncut and unopened. End papers are plain. Issued in black board slip-cover.

Published on November 26, 1927.
Edition limited to 775 numbered copies of which 750 were for sale.

This volume was printed from the same plates as the trade edition and contains the errors of that volume No. 63. The front matter varies only insofar as p. [2], instead of being blank now contains the certificate of issue and this title-page is more elaborate.

# STRANGE INTERLUDE

## 1928-1929

## 65

### FIRST EDITION

[Uniform with four volumes of collected plays — trade edition published in 1925, No. 45.]

Eugene O'Neill / [Green line] / A Play / Strange Interlude / [ Green line] / [Publisher's Device in Green] / [Green line] / New York / Boni & Liveright / 1928

[All of which is contained in green line box with decorative top and bottom.]

Collation: 8vo. [leaf measures $8\frac{1}{16}$ x $5\frac{7}{16}$ inches]; pp. 352, consisting of; p. [1], Half-title, "Strange Interlude"; p. [2], blank; p. [3], Title-page as above; p. [4], contains, "Copyright, 1928, by / Boni & Liveright, Inc. / [short line] / Printed in the United States of America" / [Permission clause for acting rights — author's agent.]; p. [5], List of Characters; p. [6], blank; p. [7], List of Acts; p. [8], blank; p. [9], Half-title, "First Part / Act One"; p. [10], blank; pp. 11-352, Text of "Strange Interlude", a play in nine acts.

Issued in binding uniform with previous volumes in the trade edition of collected works No. 45. The dust wrapper is different in design although uniform in color.

First published in February, 1928.
First printing consisted of 20,000 copies.

Error for identification:

> P. 161, l. 32-33 — Between these two lines should be inserted character identification "Evans." Although same error also in Limited Edition No. 66, it is corrected in English Edition No. 67.

# 66

## LIMITED EDITION

Strange Interlude / Eugene O'Neill / Boni & Liveright / New York / 1928 / [small dot]

*See facsimile p. 74.*

Collation: 8vo. [leaf measures 10⅛ x 7½ inches]; pp. x+ 302, consisting of; pp. [i-ii], blank; p. iii, Half title in blue, "Strange Interlude"; p. [iv], Certificate of issue with signature of author; p. [v], Title-page as above printed in blue; p. [vi], contains permission clause for acting rights — author's agent which is followed by, "Copyright, 1928, by Boni & Liveright /

# STRANGE INTERLUDE

## EUGENE O'NEILL

### BONI & LIVERIGHT
### NEW YORK
### 1928

•

(No. 66)

*Title page of the limited edition*

Printed in the United States of America"; p. [vii], List of
Characters with word "Characters" in blue; p. [viii], blank;
p. [ix], List of Acts with word "Scenes" in blue; p. [x], blank;
p. [1], Half-title in blue, "First Play"; p. [2], blank; pp.
3-[298], Text of "Strange Interlude," a play in nine acts; pp.
[299-300], blank; p. [301], Colophon; p. [302], blank.

Text is printed in blue and black to give added distinction between the thoughts and spoken words of the characters.

Issued in vellum with blue single-line border and facsimile
of author's signature in gilt on front cover. Spine has blue vellum title-label with gilt border and lettered in gilt, "Strange /
Interlude / Eugene / O'Neill." Back cover has blue border as
on front cover. Edges are uncut and unopened. End papers are
plain. Issued in buff board slip cover.

Published in March, 1928.

Edition limited to 775 numbered copies of which 750 were
for sale.

# 67

## ENGLISH EDITION

Strange Interlude / A Play by / Eugene O'Neill /
[Publisher's Device] / Jonathan Cape / Thirty
Bedford Square London / [1928]

Collation: Crown 8vo.; pp. 350.

Issued in blue cloth with facsimile signature of author in gilt
on front page. Spine of same material has lettered in gilt, "Eugene / O'Neill / [Publisher's Device] / Strange / Interlude /
Jonathan Cape" / [at top and bottom of spine is border line].
Edges are cut and end papers are plain. Issued in light yellow
dust wrapper.

First published in September, 1928.

This is the first volume on which a new style of binding is used in this O'Neill series.

# 68

# EXTRACTS FROM
# "THE STRANGE INTERLUDE"

A pamphlet, containing an unauthorized collection of extracted speeches from the play, privately published in Boston, Massachusetts presumably by "The Mayor's Committee" in September, 1929.

Collation: Leaf measures 9⅝ x 6¹¹⁄₁₆ inches; pp. 8, consisting of; pp. [1]-6, Text with caption, 'Extracts from "The Strange Interlude"' at top of p. [1]; pp. [7-8], blank.

Issued on white paper in tract form.

The speeches extracted were alleged to be obscene and the collection so made and printed was intended to supply further reason for the refusal of the City of Boston to allow the play to be produced there by the Theatre Guild of New York in September, 1929. The pamphlet was distributed to members of the clergy and to other factions prominent in the effort to maintain the impression that the play was obscene. The pamphlet was the cause of considerable controversy and it is perhaps significant that its publisher cannot be definitely identified.

*See illustration opposite.*

# EXTRACTS FROM "THE STRANGE INTERLUDE."

## FIRST ACT.

Page 14. "To the devil with sex—— our impotent pose of today to be beat on the loud drum of fornication—— eunuchs parading with the phallus."

Page 15. "prep school. ——Easter vacation—— Fatty Boggs and Jack Frazer—— that house of cheap vice—— one dollar—— why did I go—— Jack the dead game sport—— how I admired him—— afraid of the taunts—— he pointed to the Italian girl—— take her—— daring me——I went—— miserably frightened—— what a pig she was—— pretty vicious face under caked powder and rouge—— surly and contemptuous—— Lumpy body—— short legs and thick ankles—— slums of Naples——" What are you gawking about—— git a move on kid—— kid—— I was only a kid—— sixteen—— test of manhood—— ashamed to face Jack again, unless—— fool I might have lied to him."

Page 36. (Nina.) "But Gordon never possessed me——I am—— still Gordon's silly virgin—— and Gordon is muddy ashes——and I've lost my happiness forever. All that last night I knew Gordon wanted me. I knew it was only the honorable code bound Gordon who kept commanding from his brain, no you mustn't, you must respect her, you must wait until you have a marriage license."

Page 37. Gordon wanted me——I wanted Gordon——I should have made him take me. I didn't make him take me——I lost him forever——. And now I am lonely, not pregnant with anything at all but—— loathing."

## ACT TWO.

Page 73. (Marsden.) "She's hard—— like a whore—— tearing your heart out with dirty finger nails—— cruel bitch—— no kinder at heart than dollar tarts——

Page 75. (Nina.) "How could that God care about our trifling misery of death or of death. I couldn't believe in him and I wouldn't if I could. I'd rather imitate His indifference and prove that I had that one trait at least in common."

Page 80.
(Marsden.) "What do you want to be punished for Nina."
(Nina.) "For playing the silly slut, Charlie, or giving my cool clean body to men with hot hands and greedy eyes which they call love, ugh.

Page 81.
(Marsden) thinking. "Then she did—— the little filth."
(Marsden to Nina.) "Then you did—— but no Darrel."
(Nina.) No, how could I, ——the war hadn't maimed him—— there would have been no point in that. But I did with others, oh, four or five or six or seven men Charlie, ——I forget—— and it doesn't matter. They were all the same. Count them all as one and that one a ghost of nothing, that is, to me. They were important to themselves if I remember rightly. But I forget.

Page 83. (Nina.) I want children——I must become a mother so I can give myself.

(No. 68)

*Pamphlet issued in Boston as propaganda against production of the play*

# 69

ANATHEMA!

Anathema! / Litanies of Negation / By / Benjamin De Casseres / With a Foreword By / Eugene O'Neill / [Publisher's Device] / New York / Gotham Book Mart / 1928

[All of which is contained in a decorative border.]

Collation: 8vo. [leaf measures 9½ x 6¼ inches]; pp. 2 blank leaves+xii+48, consisting of; p. [i], Half-title, "Anathema! /Litanies of Negation"; p. [ii], blank; p. [iii], Title-page as above; p. [iv], Contains, "Copyright 1928 by Gotham Book Mart / Printed in U. S. A"; p. [v], Dedication, "To / Bio / Effulgent Spirit of Affirmation"; p. [vi], blank; pp. [vii]-xi, Foreword by Eugene O'Neill; p. [xii], blank; pp. [1]-44, Text of "Anathema" by Benjamin De Casseres; p. [45], Colophon with signature of author, pp. [46-48], blank.

Issued in black boards with facsimile of author's signature in silver on front cover. Spine is white parchment with the title "Anathema" lettered vertically in black, enclosed in a single line box with small decoration just above and below the box. Edges are uncut and unopened. End papers are plain. Issued in black board slip-cover.

Published in November, 1928.
Edition limited to 1250 numbered copies.

This is the first contribution to be made by O'Neill to a book published by another author.

## 70

## NEW YORK WORLD

Reproductions of two original sketches of settings for "Dynamo" on p. 2M of the New York World, a daily newspaper published in New York City, issue for February 10, 1929.

*See also No. 52.*

## DYNAMO

## 71

### FIRST EDITION

[Uniform with four volumes of collected plays — trade edition published in 1925, No. 45, except that Horace Liveright, Inc., has replaced Boni & Liveright, Inc. as publishers.]

Eugene O'Neill / [Green line] / Dynamo / [Green line] / [Publisher's Device in green] / [Green line] / New York / Horace Liveright / 1929

[All of which is contained in green line box with decorative top and bottom.]

Collation: 8vo. [leaf measures 8⅛ x 5$\frac{7}{16}$ inches]; pp. 160, consisting of; p. [1], Half-title, "Dynamo"; p. [2], blank; p. [3], Title-page as above; p. [4], Contains, "Copyright, 1929, by / Horace Liveright, Inc. / [short line] / Printed in the United States of America" / [Permission Clause for acting rights — author's agent]; p. [5], List of Characters; p. [6], blank;

pp. vii-viii, Description of setting and List of Acts and Scenes; p. [9], Half-title, "Dynamo"; p. [10], blank; pp. 11-159, Text of "Dynamo," a play in three acts; p. [160], blank.

Issued in binding uniform with previous volumes in the trade edition of collected works No. 45 except, of course, that publishers name and device have been changed on spine. The dust wrapper is different in design but still uniform in color.

First published in October, 1929.
First printing consisted of 10,000 copies.

The unusual pagination of the front matter should be noted.

Although this volume was published in advance of the English edition, No. 72, it is the third version of the play to be submitted by the author, whereas the English edition is the second version. The first was made into galley sheets from approximately the same manuscript as that used in the production of the play by the New York Theatre Guild. It never went beyond this stage. The second version was subsequently submitted by the author, set into galleys, and sent to the English publishers by the American publishers. Prior to final release by the latter of the second version, the author submitted the third version. But, in the meantime the English edition had been completed from the second version and was released in that form.

The text of the two editions is substantially different as may be seen by comparing the facsimiles of specimen pages shown here on pages 80 and 81.

## 72

### ENGLISH EDITION

Lazarus Laughed / And / Dynamo / Two Plays by / Eugene O'Neill / [Publisher's Device] / Jonathan Cape Ltd / Thirty Bedford Square, London / [1929]

MRS. FIFE. Warn you about what, Reuben?

REUBEN. That I was living in sin—that Dynamo would never find me worthy of her secret until I'd given up the flesh and purified myself! (*Then proudly.*) And I found the strength to do it. It was hard! I was beginning to really love Ada.

MRS. FIFE (*simply*). Of course, you love Ada—and you shouldn't act so mean to her, Reuben. You haven't been around in a month or more. She's making herself sick worrying.

REUBEN (*intensely*). I'd like to see her! I'd love to! But I can't! Don't you understand I can't—that my finding the secret is more important than—but when I come back bringing peace and happiness to the world it will mean peace and happiness for Ada and me too! Everything will be all right then!

(*Then thinking with sudden fear and doubt.*) But supposing the miracle doesn't happen to-night? . . . have I got to go on and on like this? . . . Ada keeps coming to me every night in dreams . . . the temptation of her body . . . I've beaten myself with my belt till the pain drove it off . . . but I can't keep on much longer . . .

(*He sways dizzily on his feet, passing his hand over his eyes—then straightens himself and turns to Mrs. Fife.*) I've got to go in. They'll be missing me. You'll stay around, won't you? (*He*

85

(No. 72)

*Specimen page from the English edition.*
*Start at line 14 on this page and at line 1 on opposite page*
*and note variations in text*

you understand I can't—that my finding the secret is more important than—?

> [*Then thinking with sudden fear and doubt*]
> But supposing the miracle doesn't happen to-night? . . . Ada keeps coming in dreams . . . her body . . . I've beaten myself with my belt . . . I can't keep on much longer . . .
> [*He sways dizzily on his feet, passing his hand over his eyes—then straightens himself and turns to* MRS. FIFE]

I've got to go in. They'll be missing me. And I've got to pray to her.

> [*He goes to the door*]

You wait until your husband's gone home. Then you come in.

MRS. FIFE

All right, Reuben.

> [REUBEN *slides back the dynamo-room door a few feet and enters, closing it behind him.* MRS. FIFE *stares after him mooningly*] [*A moment later the door from the dynamo room is opened again and* FIFE *comes out, closing it behind him. He hasn't changed since his last appearance. He starts to walk hesitatingly off right—then stops without looking around him and does not notice his wife*]

[ 136 ]

Collation: 8vo. [leaf measures 7½ x 4¾ inches]; pp. 150+ 106, [each play having separate pagination], consisting of; p. [1], Half-title, "Lazarus Laughed/and/Dynamo"; p. [2], contains, "By the same author / [small solid star] / The Emperor Jones / The Moon of the Caribbees / The Hairy Ape / Anna Christie / Beyond the Horizon / All God's Chillun Got Wings/The Great God Brown/Marco Millions/Strange Interlude"; p. [3], Title-page as above; p. [4], contains, "First Published MCMXXIX / Printed in Great Britain by / Butler & Tanner Ltd/Frome"; p. [5], Half-title, "Lazarus Laughed /(1925-1926)/A Play for an Imaginative Theatre"; p. [6], blank; p. 7, List of Acts and Scenes; p. 8, List of Characters; pp. 9-150, Text of "Lazarus Laughed"; p. [1], Half-title, "Dynamo"; p. [2], List of Characters; pp. 3-4 Description of Setting and List of Acts and Scenes; pp. 5-102, Text of "Dynamo"; pp. [103-106], blank.

Issued in blue cloth with facsimile signature of author in gilt on front cover. Spine of same material has lettered in gilt, "Eugene / O'Neill / [Publisher's Device] / Lazarus / Laughed / Jonathan Cape"/[At top and bottom of spine is border line.] Edges are cut and end papers are plain. Issued in light yellow dust wrapper.

First published in November, 1929.

*Uniform with No. 67.*

See note of variations between English and American editions No. 71.

# 73

## LIMITED EDITION

Dynamo / Eugene O'Neill / Horace Liveright / New York / 1929

Collation: 8vo. [leaf measures 10⅛ x 7½ inches] ; pp. viii+ 152 [two additional leaves at front — first of which is blank, recto of second leaf has certificate of issue with signature of author, and verso is blank], consisting of; p. [i], Half-title in blue, "Dynamo"; p. [ii], blank; p. [iii], Title-page as above printed in blue; p. [iv], contains permission clause for acting rights — authors agent, and below which is, "Copyright, 1929, by Horace Liveright, Inc. / Printed in the United States of America"; p. [v], List of Characters with the word "Characters" in blue; p. [vi], blank; pp. vii-viii, Description of Setting and List of Acts and Scenes with heading in blue; p. [1], Half-title in blue, "Act One"; p. [2], blank; pp. 3-151, Text of "Dynamo", a play in three acts; p. [152], Colophon.

Text is printed in blue and black — as in No. 66 — to give added distinction between the thoughts and the spoken words of the characters.

Issued in blue-green vellum with facsimile signature of author in gilt on front cover. Spine has white title label which has border of single gilt line within which is lettered in gilt, "Dynamo / Eugene / O'Neill". Edges are uncut and unopened. End papers are plain. Issued in purple board slip cover.

Published in December, 1929.

Edition limited to 775 numbered copies of which 750 were for sale.

# PART TWO

# CRITICAL MATTER ON O'NEILL
# UNPUBLISHED PLAYS
# ANTHOLOGIES.

BOOKS containing
Articles on–
or Reference to–
Eugene O'Neill

### 1917

THE LITTLE THEATRE IN THE UNITED STATES. Constance D. Mackay. New York.

### 1919

COMEDIANS ALL. George J. Nathan. New York.

### 1920

THE BEST PLAYS OF 1919-1920. Burns Mantle. Boston.
SEEN ON THE STAGE. Clayton Hamilton. New York.

### 1921

THE BEST PLAYS OF 1920-1921. Burns Mantle. Boston.
A STUDY COURSE IN MODERN DRAMA. Elizabeth Lay. (University of North Carolina Extension Leaflets.) Chapel Hill, N. C.

THE THEATRE? THE DRAMA? THE GIRLS. George J. Nathan. New York.

THE THEATRE OF TOMORROW. Kenneth Macgowan. New York.

### 1922

APPRAISEMENTS AND ASPERITIES. Felix E. Schelling. Philadelphia.

THE BEST PLAYS OF 1921-1922. Burns Mantle. Boston.

THE DRAMA OF TRANSITION. Isaac Goldberg. Cincinnati.

*Plays: First Series*, Introduction to. C. E. Bechhofer. London.

SHOUTS AND MURMURS. Alexander Woollcott. New York.

### 1923

THE CRAFTSMANSHIP OF THE ONE-ACT PLAY. Percival Wilde. Boston.

THE LITERARY RENAISSANCE IN AMERICA. C. E. Bechhofer. London (N. Y., 1923.)

*The Moon of The Caribbees*, Introduction to. St. John Ervine. London.

*The Moon of The Caribbees*, Introduction to. George J. Nathan. Modern Library No. 111. New York.

OUR AMERICAN THEATRE. Oliver M. Saylor. New York.

SOME MODERN AUTHORS. S. B. P. Mais. London (N. Y., 1923.)

THE WORLD IN FALSEFACE. George J. Nathan. New York.

### 1924

THE CONTEMPORARY THEATRE, 1923. James Agate. London.

CONVERSATIONS ON CONTEMPORARY DRAMA. Clayton Hamilton. New York.

MATERIA CRITICA. George J. Nathan. New York.

ENCHANTED AISLES. Alexander Woollcott. New York.

PORTRAITS: REAL AND IMAGINARY. Ernest Boyd. New York.

SOME CONTEMPORARY AMERICANS. Percy H. Boynton. Chicago.

SOME CONTEMPORARY DRAMATISTS. Graham Sutton. London
(N. Y., 1924.)

A STUDY COURSE IN AMERICAN ONE-ACT PLAYS. Ethel T. Rock-
well. (University of North Carolina Extension Leaflets.)
Chapel Hill, N. C.

THE YOUNGEST DRAMA. Ashley Dukes. London (Chicago,
1924.)

## 1925

THE AMERICAN DRAMATIST. Montrose J. Moses. Boston.

THE ART THEATRE. Sheldon Cheney. New York.

THE BEST PLAYS OF 1924-1925. Burns Mantle. Boston.

THE CONTEMPORARY THEATRE, 1924. James Agate. London.

DRAMATISTS OF THE NEW AMERICAN THEATRE. Thomas H.
Dickinson. New York.

THE AUTOBIOGRAPHY OF AN ATTITUDE. George J. Nathan.
New York.

PROVINCETOWN AND MACDOUGALL STREET? A Preface to
"Greek Coins" by George Cram Cook. Edna Kenton.
New York.

A STUDY OF THE MODERN DRAMA. Barrett H. Clark. New
York.

THE TECHNIQUE OF THE ONE-ACT PLAY. Robert L. Gannon.
New York.

TROUBADOUR. Alfred Kreymborg. New York.

WRITING THE ONE-ACT PLAY. Harold N. Hildebrand. New
York.

### 1926

THE BEST PLAYS OF 1925-1926. Burns Mantle. Boston.

EUGENE O'NEILL. Barrett H. Clark. (Revised in 1929.) New York.

THE HOUSE OF SATAN. George J. Nathan. New York.

THE THEATRE OF GEORGE J. NATHAN. Isaac Goldberg. New York.

### 1927

THE BEST PLAYS OF 1926-1927. Burns Mantle. New York.

FIRE UNDER THE ANDES. Elizabeth S. Sergeant. New York.

A HISTORY OF THE AMERICAN DRAMA FROM THE CIVIL WAR TO THE PRESENT DAY. Vol. 2. Arthur H. Quinn. New York.

THE PLAYS OF EUGENE O'NEILL. A. F. White. (Studies by Members of the Faculty, Vol. 26. Western Reserve University.) Cleveland, Ohio.

THE ROAD TO THE TEMPLE. Susan Glaspell. New York.

### 1928

THE ART OF EUGENE O'NEILL. Joseph T. Shipley. Seattle, Wash.

ART OF THE NIGHT. George J. Nathan. New York.

THE BEST PLAYS OF 1927-1928. Burns Mantle. New York.

THE DEVELOPMENT OF DRAMATIC ART. Donald C. Stuart. New York.

*The Emperor Jones and The Straw*, Introduction to. Dudley Nichols. Modern Library No. 146. New York.

THE HISTORIC SIGNIFICANCE OF O'NEILL'S *Strange Interlude*. Harry Waton. New York.

MODERN DRAMATIC STRUCTURE. Dorothy J. Kaucher. Columbia, Mo.

SIXTEEN AUTHORS TO ONE. David Karsner. New York.

SPOKESMEN. T. K. Whipple. New York.

## 1929

AMERICAN PLAYWRIGHTS OF TODAY. Burns Mantle. New York.

THE BEST PLAYS OF 1928-1929. Burns Mantle. New York.

CONTEMPORARY AMERICAN LITERATURE. John M. Manly and Edith Rickert. Revised Edition. New York.

EUGENE O'NEILL, THE MAN AND HIS PLAYS. Barrett H. Clark. New York.

SIX PLAYS OF EUGENE O'NEILL. Alan D. Mickle. London (N. Y., 1929.)

THE THEATRE GUILD. Walter P. Eaton. New York.

## 1930

AMERICAN AND BRITISH LITERATURE SINCE 1890. Carl Van Doren. New York.

AN HOUR OF AMERICAN DRAMA. Barrett H. Clark. Philadelphia.

UPSTAGE. John M. Brown. New York.

## 1931

THE TESTAMENT OF A CRITIC. George J. Nathan. New York.

### PERIODICALS
#### containing Articles on
#### Eugene O'Neill

(Reviews of plays as published or produced are too numerous and too variable to be included in this list of critical articles.)

*The American Magazine, N. Y.*

THE EXTRAORDINARY STORY OF EUGENE O'NEILL. Mary B. Mullett. November, 1922.

*The American Mercury, N. Y.*

O'NEILL'S LATEST. George J. Nathan. February, 1926.

O'NEILL'S FINEST PLAY. George J. Nathan. July, 1927.

AN ESTIMATE OF EUGENE O'NEILL. George G. Nathan. April, 1928.

A NON-CONDUCTOR. George J. Nathan. March, 1929.

*Arts Gazette, London*

A NEW AMERICAN DRAMATIST. Barrett H. Clark. May, 1919.

*The Bookman, N. Y.*

ENTER EUGENE O'NEILL. Pierre Loving. August, 1921.

THE GREAT GOD O'NEILL. Winifred Katzkin. September, 1928.

*The Century Magazine, N. Y.*

THE REAL EUGENE O'NEILL. O. M. Saylor. January, 1922.

*The Contemporary Review, London*

THE PLAYS OF EUGENE O'NEILL. Andrew F. Malone. March, 1926.

*Country Life in America, N. Y.*

HOME ON THE DUNES. J. M. Breese. November, 1923.

*Drama, N. Y.*

THE WORK OF EUGENE O'NEILL. O. M. Saylor. March, 1921.

A BROADWAY PHILOSOPHER. Jack R. Crawford. January, 1922.

EUGENE O'NEILL AND THE GUILD. Barrett H. Clark. March, 1928.

BEYOND *Strange Interlude*. Harry McGuire. March, 1929.

*Strange Interlude* AND THE BLAH BROTHERHOOD. Alice E. Philipps. March, 1929.

*The Dublin Magazine, Dublin*

THE PLAYS OF EUGENE O'NEILL. Vol. 7, 1923.

*Everybody's Magazine, N. Y.*

THE RISE OF EUGENE O'NEILL. Alexander Woollcott. June, 1920.

*Figure in the Carpet, N. Y.*

THE TRAGEDY OF O'NEILL. Elva de Pue. May, 1928.


*Fortnightly Review, London*

THE PLAYS OF EUGENE O'NEILL. E. A. Baughan. May, 1923.


*Greenwich Village Playbill, N. Y.*

EUGENE O'NEILL IN EUROPE. Rudolf Kummer. Bill No. 2, Season of 1924-1925.


*The Hound and Horn, Portland, Me.*

EUGENE O'NEILL. Francis Ferguson. Winter, 1930.


*The Industrial Pioneer, Chicago*

THE EMPEROR O'NEILL. Bob Robbins. January, 1925.


*International Book Review (Literary Digest), N. Y.*

HOW EUGENE O'NEILL CAME OUT OF THE DEPTHS. B. De-Casseres. November, 1926.


*Journal of Outdoor Life, N. Y.*

WHAT A SANATORIUM DID FOR EUGENE O'NEILL. J. F. O'Neill. June, 1923.


*The Living Age, N. Y.*

AN AMERICAN DRAMATIST ABROAD. Anonymous. July 8, 1922.
AMERICAN TRAGEDY IN EUROPE. Anonymous. November 28, 1925.

### *The Nation, N. Y.*

THE DEVELOPMENT OF EUGENE O'NEILL. Ludwig Lewisohn. March 22, 1922.

*Anna Christie* in Russia. V. Vetlinguin. March 4, 1925.

### *The New Republic, N. Y.*

AN ESTIMATE OF EUGENE O'NEILL. Stark Young. November 15, 1922.

THE TRAGEDY OF EUGENE O'NEILL. T. K. Whipple. January 21, 1925.

O'NEILL — THE MAN WITH A MASK. E. S. Sergeant. March 16, 1927.

### *The New Statesman, London*

AN AMERICAN DRAMATIST AND SOME PLAYERS. S. K. Ratcliffe. July 9, 1921.

### *New York Evening Post*

EUGENE O'NEILL — A PLAYWRIGHT NOT WITHOUT HONOR. Anonymous. January 7, 1928.

### *New York Herald-Tribune*

EUGENE O'NEILL TALKS OF HIS OWN PLAYS. Anonymous. November 16, 1924.

THE HERMIT OF CAPE COD. W. P. Eaton. January 8, 1928.

REALISM DOOMED, O'NEILL BELIEVES. Richard Watts, Jr. February 5, 1928.

THE REAL BACKGROUND OF O'NEILL IN HIS *S. S. Glencairn* GROUP. Barrett H. Clark. February 10, 1929.

DOWN TO THE SEA. Anonymous. March 3, 1929.

CAN O'NEILL DO WRONG OR NOT? A Query That Requires a
Reply. Richard Watts, Jr. March 19, 1929.

### New York Sun

THE PLAYS OF EUGENE O'NEILL. Barrett H. Clark. May 18,
1919.

A EUGENE O'NEILL MISCELLANY. Anonymous. January 12,
1928.

EUGENE O'NEILL. Sidney Skolsky. (The Times Square Tin-
Types.) May 13, 1929.

### New York Telegram

(UNTITLED ARTICLE.) Heywood Broun. February 14, 1929.

### New York Times

O'NEILL IN PARIS. M. A. B. November 18, 1923.

EUGENE O'NEILL AS A REALIST. Kenneth Macgowan. March
23, 1924.

O'NEILL DEFENDS HIS PLAY OF NEGRO LIFE. Louis Kantor.
May 11, 1924.

O'NEILL LIFTS THE CURTAIN ON HIS EARLY DAYS. Louis Kalo-
dyme. December 21, 1924.

NEW O'NEILL ASPECTS. J. Brooks Atkinson. December 20,
1925.

IBSEN AND O'NEILL. J. Brooks Atkinson. January 31, 1926.

O'NEILL IN HIS OWN PLAYS. Kenneth Macgowan. January 9,
1927.

MAN'S CHALLENGE TO DEATH IN *Lazarus Laughed*. J. Brooks
Atkinson. November 27, 1927.

O'NEILL AND HIS PLAYS. Anonymous. January 8, 1928.

O'NEILL STIRS THE GODS OF THE DRAMA. H. I. Brock. January 15, 1928.

*Strange Interlude.* J. Brooks Atkinson. February 5, 1928.

HONOR ENOUGH FOR EVERYBODY. J. Brooks Atkinson. January 27, 1929.

CONCLUDING A DRAMATIC CYCLE. J. Brooks Atkinson. February 17, 1929.

### New York Tribune

EUGENE O'NEILL'S CREDO AND HIS REASONS FOR HIS FAITH. Anonymous, but alleged to have been written by O'Neill. February 13, 1921.

### New York World

BACK TO THE SOURCE OF PLAYS WRITTEN BY EUGENE O'NEILL. Charles P. Sweeney. November 9, 1924.

EUGENE O'NEILL IN BERLIN. C. Hooper Trask. January 4, 1925.

I KNEW HIM WHEN - - - . John V. A. Weaver. February 21, 1926.

SOUR, FAULT-FINDING CRITICS ARE NEEDED. Heywood Broun. January 15, 1928.

MR. HECHT GOES FOR *Strange Interlude.* Alexander Woollcott. May 14, 1928.

### The Observer, London

MR. EUGENE O'NEILL. St. John Ervine. October 9, 1921.

MR. ROBERT NICHOLS AND MR. EUGENE O'NEILL. St. John Ervine. June 11, 1922.

*Anna Christie* IN PRINT. St. John Ervine. May 27, 1923.

MR. EUGENE O'NEILL. St. John Ervine. October 31, 1926.

*The Public Ledger, Philadelphia*

MAKING PLAYS WITH A TRAGIC END. An Intimate Interview with Eugene O'Neill Who Tells Why He Does It. Malcolm Mollan. January 22, 1922.

*Poet Lore, Boston*

STRINDBERG'S INFLUENCE ON EUGENE O'NEILL. Ira N. Hayward. Winter, 1928.

*Popular Biography, N. Y.*

EUGENE O'NEILL — A VIGNETTE. B. DeCasseres. April, 1930.

*Provincetown Playbill, N. Y.*

EUGENE O'NEILL, ABLE SEAMAN. Louis Kantor. Bill No. 2, Season of 1924-1925.

*Scribner's Magazine, N. Y.*

THE SIGNIFICANCE OF RECENT AMERICAN DRAMA. Arthur H. Quinn. July, 1922.

EUGENE O'NEILL, POET AND MYSTIC. Arthur H. Quinn. October, 1926.

*Shadowland, N. Y.*

THE ARTIST OF THE THEATRE. O. M. Saylor. April, 1922.

*The Spectator, London*

THE DRAMATIST OF MONOMANIA. Anonymous. October 17, 1925.

*The Theatre, N. Y.*

PERSONALITY PORTRAITS — EUGENE O'NEILL. Alta M. Coleman. April, 1920.

*Theatre Arts Magazine (and Monthly), N. Y.*

EUGENE O'NEILL. W. P. Eaton. October, 1920.

EUGENE O'NEILL AND THIS BIG BUSINESS OF BROADWAY. Robert Garland. January, 1925.

EUGENE O'NEILL. Barrett H. Clark. May, 1926.

*Theatre Guild Quarterly (and Magazine), N. Y.*

SOME NOTES ON THE PRODUCTION OF O'NEILL's *Strange Interlude*. Philip Moeller. February, 1928.

THE O'NEILL SOLILOQUY. Kenneth Macgowan. February, 1929.

*Theatre Magazine, N. Y.*

EUGENE O'NEILL — THE INNER MAN. Carol Bird. June, 1924.

OUR NATIVE DRAMATIST COMES INTO HIS OWN — EUGENE O'NEILL. Grenville Vernon. May, 1925.

EUGENE O'NEILL — HIS PLACE IN THE SUN. Hilma Enander. January, 1926.

IS HIS POWER IN DECLINE? St. John Ervine. May, 1926.

EUGENE O'NEILL IN THE ASCENDENT. F. H. Freed. October, 1926.

EUGENE O'NEILL — FROM CARDIFF TO XANADU. B. DeCasseres. August, 1927.

THE TRIUMPHANT GENIUS OF EUGENE O'NEILL. B. DeCasseres. February, 1928.

OUT OF PROVINCETOWN. Harry Kemp. April, 1930.

*Vanity Fair, N. Y.*

THE THEATRICAL CALLBOARD. Kenneth Macgowan. April, 1922.

GIVING O'NEILL TILL IT HURTS. Alexander Woollcott. February, 1928.

THE NEWER O'NEILL. G. Gabriel. April, 1928.

STRANGE INTERVIEW. John Riddell (Corey Ford). May, 1928.

*Vogue, N. Y.*

AN APPRECIATION OF EUGENE O'NEILL. Carb. September 15, 1926.

*The World's Work, N. Y.*

THE AMERICAN DRAMA FLOWERS — EUGENE O'NEILL AS A GREAT PLAYWRIGHT. W. P. Eaton. November, 1926.

*World Today, N. Y.*

EUGENE O'NEILL AS A GREAT PLAYWRIGHT. W. P. Eaton. February, 1927.

*Yale Review, New Haven, Conn.*

O'NEILL'S FIRST DECADE. George P. Baker. July, 1926.

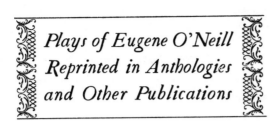

## Plays of Eugene O'Neill Reprinted in Anthologies and Other Publications

*Before Breakfast*

A TREASURY OF PLAYS FOR WOMEN, edited by Frank Shay. Boston, 1922.

*Beyond the Horizon*

REPRESENTATIVE AMERICAN PLAYS, edited by Arthur H. Quinn. Revised Edition, New York, 1925.

*Bound East for Cardiff*

PROVINCETOWN PLAYS, edited by George Cram Cook and Frank Shay. Cincinnati, 1921.

*Moon of The Caribbees and Six Other Plays of the Sea.* Modern Library, No. 111, New York, 1923.

THE AMERICAN SCENE, edited by Barrett H. Clark and Kenyon Nicholson. New York, 1930.

*The Dreamy Kid*

PLAYS OF NEGRO LIFE, edited by Alain L. Locke and Montgomery Gregory. New York, 1927.

PLAYS OF AMERICAN LIFE AND FANTASY, edited by Edith J. R. Isaacs. New York, 1929.

### The Emperor Jones

CONTEMPORARY AMERICAN PLAYS, edited by Arthur H. Quinn. New York, 1923.

REPRESENTATIVE AMERICAN DRAMAS, NATIONAL AND LOCAL, edited by Montrose J. Moses. Boston, 1925.

THE GOLDEN BOOK MAGAZINE. New York, April, 1926.

EVERYBODY'S MAGAZINE. New York, April, 1926.

AN INTRODUCTION TO DRAMA, edited by Jay B. Hubbell and John O. Beatty. New York, 1927.

PLAYS OF NEGRO LIFE, edited by Alain L. Locke and Montgomery Gregory. New York, 1927.

*The Emperor Jones and The Straw.* Modern Library, No. 146, New York, 1928.

CHIEF CONTEMPORARY DRAMATISTS — Third Series — edited by Thomas H. Dickinson. Boston, 1930.

### The Hairy Ape

CONTEMPORARY DRAMA: ENGLISH AND AMERICAN, edited by Thomas H. Dickinson and Jack R. Crawford. Boston, 1925.

### Ile

FIFTY CONTEMPORARY ONE-ACT PLAYS, edited by Frank Shay and Pierre Loving. Cincinnati, 1920.

THE ATLANTIC BOOK OF MODERN PLAYS, edited by Sterling A. Leonard. Boston, 1921.

*Moon of The Caribbees and Six Other Plays of the Sea.* Modern Library, No. 111, New York, 1923.

ONE-ACT PLAYS, edited by George A. Goldstone. Boston, 1926.

DRAMAS BY PRESENT-DAY WRITERS, edited by Raymond W. Pence. New York, 1927.

THE GOLDEN BOOK MAGAZINE. New York, February, 1929.

ONE-ACT PLAYS, edited by Barrett H. Clark and Thomas R. Cook. Boston, 1929.

### In the Zone

REPRESENTATIVE ONE-ACT PLAYS BY AMERICAN AUTHORS, edited by Margaret Mayorga. Boston, 1919.

*Moon of The Caribbees and Six Other Plays of the Sea.* Modern Library, No. 111, New York, 1923.

### The Long Voyage Home

*Moon of The Caribbees and Six Other Plays of the Sea.* Modern Library, No. 111, New York, 1923.

### The Moon of the Caribbees

*The Moon of The Caribbees and Six Other Plays of the Sea.* Modern Library, No. 111, New York, 1923.

FIFTY MORE CONTEMPORARY ONE-ACT PLAYS, edited by Frank Shay. New York, 1928.

### The Rope

*The Moon of The Caribbees and Six Other Plays of the Sea.* Modern Library, No. 111, New York, 1923.

### The Straw

*The Emperor Jones and The Straw.* Modern Library, No. 146, New York, 1928.

*Where the Cross Begins*

*The Moon of The Caribbees and Six Other Plays of the Sea.* Modern Library, No. 111, New York, 1923.

A BOOK OF MODERN PLAYS, edited by George R. Coffman. Chicago, 1925.

MORE ONE-ACT PLAYS, edited by Helen L. Cohen. New York, 1927.

TWELVE ONE-ACT PLAYS FOR STUDY AND PRODUCTION, edited by S. Marion Tucker. Boston, 1929.

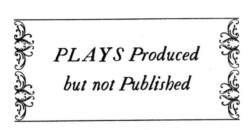

## PLAYS Produced
### but not Published

THE SNIPER. One act. Written in 1915. Produced by the Provincetown Players, 1917.

CHRIS. Three acts, six scenes. (Early version — also under other titles — of *Anna Christie*). Written in 1919. Produced in Atlantic City, N. J., 1920.

EXORCISM. One act. Written in 1919. Produced by the Provincetown Players, 1920.

THE ANCIENT MARINER. One act. Written in 1923. Produced by the Provincetown Plays, 1924.

*PART THREE*

COLLECTED POEMS
BY
O'NEILL

## AN EXPLANATION

The reader is requested to remember that the following poems are examples of Mr. O'Neill's earliest work and that he was extremely reluctant to have them reprinted. However, he has graciously given his consent in order that this record might be complete.

*P O E M S*

## FREE

### By Eugene G. O'Neill

Weary am I of the tumult, sick of the staring crowd,
Pining for wild sea places where the soul may think aloud.
Fled is the glamour of cities, dead as the ghost of a dream,
While I pine anew for the tint of blue on the breast of the old
    Gulf Stream.

I have had my dance with Folly, nor do I shirk the blame;
I have sipped the so-called Wine of Life and paid the price of
    shame;
But I know that I shall find surcease, the rest my spirit craves,
Where the rainbows play in the flying spray,
'Mid the keen salt kiss of the waves.

Then it's ho! for the plunging deck of a bark, the hoarse song
    of the crew,
With never a thought of those we left or what we are going
    to do;
Nor heed the old ship's burning, but break the shackles of care
And at last be free, on the open sea, with the trade wind in our
    hair.

(Pleiades Club Year Book for 1912. See No. 1)

## FRATRICIDE

By Eugene G. O'Neill

The call resounds on every hand,
   The loud, exultant call to arms.
With patriotic blare of band
   It quickens, pulses, rouses, charms;
Mouthing it's insolent command:
   "Come, let us rob our neighbor's farms."

Alas, what salve does conscience need
   When love of country's the pretense?
We must demand by force of deed
   The peon's scant remaining pence;
Nor see his misery, nor heed
   His wail of anguished impotence.

But who shall fight this holy war?
   Surely the servants of the great,
Those servile cringers at the door,
   Those parasites who fawn and wait,
Into whose clutching fingers pour
   The crumbs, the favors of the State.

Doubtless the bipeds of this breed
　Will be the first to join the hunt;
For lust of gold will fight and bleed,
　Will gladly bear the battle's brunt.
The cannon's hungry mouth will feed
　Upon them crowding to the front.

Ho, ho, my friend, and think you so?
　And have you not read history?
This much of war, at least, we know:
　The jingoes are the first to flee.
The plutocrats who cause the woe
　Are arrogant but cowardly.

They sow the wind, they watch it grow;
　With eager breath they fan the flame.
Fine indignation makes them glow.
　They rant about their country's fame.
They prate of liberty (you know
　That's part and parcel of the game).

But who is then the whirlwind's prey
　Since these foul curs turn tail and fly?
Who pays the price that some must pay?
　Whose widows mourn, whose orphans cry?
The poor? The poor who must obey,
　The poor who only live to die.

The army of the poor must fight,
　New taxes come to crush them down.
They feel the iron fist of Might
　Press on their brows the thorny crown.
They see the oily smile of Right.
　They don the sacrificial gown.

With ringing cheers they are led out,
 Poor sheep, to slay their brother sheep.
They are silent — only jingoes shout,
 And only wives and children weep.
What matter victory or rout
 So it brings on the final sleep!

Their shepherds bless them as they wait
 With unctuous platitudes inane.
With words of God instilling hate
 They slink off calling on his name
To polish the collection plate
 (For Christ was crucified in vain).

Scorched by the blazing tropic sun
 Some die of fever, some are shot.
In battles lost and battles won
 They give their lives and are forgot.
They die off slowly one by one.
 Their thin, unburied bodies rot.

At last a crowning victory;
 Then peace. Poor heroes all unnamed
The sad-eyed remnant home from sea
 Are cheered, and for a day are famed,
Then cast back into misery
 With weakened bodies sick and maimed.

For they must live and they must eat;
 Their families are hungry, too.
Back to the dark, foul-smelling street,
 The ruthless toil begins anew
Slave for a tainted bite of meat!
 The factory shambles claim their due.

Glory is weak, unwholesome fare
  For those who cry for lack of bread.
The war is over; who shall care
  If they be given stones instead?
With paltry pensions we shall dare
  To pay the women for their dead.

\*　\*　\*　\*　\*　\*

"A good war haloes any cause."
  What war could halo this cause, pray?
The wise man's words had given pause
  To him, were he alive today
To see by what unholy laws
  The plutocrats extend their sway.

What cause could be more asinine
  Than yours, ye slaves of bloody toil?
Is not your bravery sublime
  Beneath a tropic sun to broil
And bleed and groan — for Guggenheim!
  And give your lives for — Standard Oil!

Noble indeed to think your loot
  Is robbery of a brother's whole
Store of a lifetime. Brave, to boot,
  To play the skulking butcher's role.
For every peon that you shoot
  A brother's death will stain your soul.

Go, tell the wan-faced, weeping wives
   The tale of your victorious war!
Gladden the lonely orphan lives
   With tales of smelters, wells galore!
Picture the happiness of Dives! —
   The poor are poorer than before.

Comrades, awaken to new birth!
   New values on the tables write!
What is your vaunted courage worth
   Unless you rise up in your might
And cry: "All workers on the earth
   Are brothers and WE WILL NOT FIGHT!"

(New York Call, May 17, 1914. See No. 3)

# SPEAKING, TO THE SHADE OF DANTE, OF BEATRICES.

"Lo, even I am Beatrice!"
    That line keeps singing in my bean.
I feel the same ecstatic bliss
    As did the fluent Florentine
Who heard the well-known hell-flame hiss.

Dante, your damozel was tall
    And lean and sad — I've seen her face
On many a best-parlor wall —
    I don't think she was such an ace.
She doesn't class with mine at all.

Her eyes were not so large or grey;
    She had no such heart-teasing smile,
Or hair so beautiful; and say,
    I hate to state it, but her style
Would never get her by today.

I'm not denying that your queen
    In your eyes may have been a bear.
You couldn't pull the stuff I've seen
    About her, if she wasn't there —
That soft poetic bull, I mean.

But just to call your rhythmic bluff
   I'll say, before I ring the bell
And kill this roundelay of fluff,
   Like Dante, I'd go plumtoel
For Beatrice — and that's enough!

— E. O'N.

(In "The Conning Tower" — New York Tribune, July 5, 1915.
See No. 5.)

## SUBMARINE

My soul is a submarine.
My aspirations are torpedoes.
I will hide unseen
Beneath the surface of life
Watching for ships,
Dull, heavy-laden merchant ships,
Rust-eaten, grimy galeons of commerce
Wallowing with obese assurance,
Too sluggish to fear or wonder,
Mocked by the laughter of waves ,
And the spit of disdainful spray.

I will destroy them
Because the sea is beautiful.

That is why I lurk
Menacingly
In green depths.

                              —(Unsigned)

(The Masses, February, 1917. See No. 9)

## NEW LONDON TELEGRAPH

(The following poems are all contributions made to the column, "Laconics" in the New London Telegraph, August to December, 1912.)

## THE WATERWAYS CONVENTION

### A Study in Prophecy

(With apologies to Hiawatha)

O the conning and the bulling!
O the bulling and the conning!
Those three golden days of summer,
When the Waterways Convention
Came at last to old New London.
Chieftans from far distant regions
Came to test our festal welcome,
Came and spoke, and then departed.
Spoke of what they knew, and often —
Wisely spoke of what they knew not.
O the welcome that we gave them!
How we tendered them the glad hand!
How we dined and even wined them!
Feasts and races and receptions!
Took the lid right off our prices.
Let them soar way up to heaven.
Saying sagely "For safe keeping
You had better leave your wampum
In the city of New London."

Hitherward came Big Bill Taftus,
Chieftan of our mighty nation
Faint hope of the Grand Old Party
With an eye for snaring voters.
Big he was in point of body,
And his words were even bigger
When he spoke about the future
Of our dear old Whaling village.
Spoke about our glorious future
(With an eye for snaring voters).

Brothers we shall all remember
How before the whole convention
Gravely spoke our chief Mahanus,
Sachem of the tribe of Whalers,
Blessed with gift of divination
He removed the veil of Isis,
Peered into the misty future,
Sketched with rare prophetic sureness
The New London of the future.

"Thirty story office buildings
We will see the length of State street.
We will take the "tube" to Groton
And the subway clear to Noank,
Or the "L" to Oswagatchie.
We will gather at the new docks
To see off the Lusitania.
And our bay will be so crowded
We will have a traffic policeman
Rowing beats upon the waters.
And we'll have an adding expert
To keep track of the collisions.

A Stock Exchange will be on Main street
And the Capitol we'll pilfer
From the puny grasp of Hartford.
We will then produce our great men.
Envy not New York it's Becker
We will have a greater grafter.
We will have our bands of "gun men"
"Gyp the Bloods" and "Lefty Louies"
And mayhap — the gods propitious —
We will even have a Thaw trial.
Property will rise in value
Till we're all so rich, my brothers,
That our heirs will try to slip some
Cyanide into our porridge."

Here the sachem of our city
Paused to make his words more weighty;
Quoth he "All we need is wampum
All we need is the dinero"
And at this the whole convention
Rose and shouted as one body
"All we all need is the wampum."

—Eugene O'Neill.

(August 26, 1912)

## VILLANELLE OF YE YOUNG POET'S FIRST VILLANELLE TO HIS LADYE AND YE DIFFICULTIES THEREOF

To sing the charms of Rosabelle,
To pour my soul out at her feet,
I try to write this villanelle.

Now I am caught within her spell,
It seems to me most wonderous sweet
To sing the charms of Rosabelle.

I seek in vain for words to tell
My love — Alas, my muse is weak!
I try to write this villanelle.

Would I had power to compel
The English language incomplete
To sing the charms of Rosabelle.

The ardent thoughts that in me dwell
On paper I would fain repeat
I try to write this villanelle.

My effort fruitless is. O H - - 1!
I'll tell her all when next we meet.
To sing the charms of Rosabelle,
I tried to write this villanelle.

— Eugene O'Neill.

(August 27, 1912)

## BALLARD OF OLD GIRLS

Where is Cora the corn-fed girlie?
   Idol of mine in the bare-foot days,
Whose laughing summons awoke me early
   To "hide and seek" in the woodland ways.
Where is the heroine of the plays?
   Who mocked my first calf-love, I fear;
Probably playing the "Four-a-days"!
   "But where are the snows of yester year?"

Where is Edith the prep-school beauty?
   Whose notes I found in a chink of the wall
Letters of love addressed to "Cutie"
   Answered by "Light of my soul", "My all"
Where is the "widow" of Nassau Hall?
   Always there with the college cheer,
Yours in springtime and mine in fall
   "But where are the snows of yester year?"

Where are Betty and Maud and Mabel?
   Chorus ladies that cared for wine,
With appetites o'erwhelmingly able,
   Leaving you skinned to a last lone dime
Where's May the queen of the burlesque "time"?
   Not averse to a schooner of beer,
Tipping the scales at two hundred and nine,
   "But where are the snows of yester year?"

Let me not ask where they are gone
Forgotten am I by them all I fear
The future calls with its witching song
"But where are the snows of yester year?"

—E. O.
(August 28, 1912)

## (Untitled)

"(With apologies to J. W. Riley)"

Our Teddy opens wide his mouth,
  N'runs around n'yells all day,
N'calls some people naughty names,
  N'says things that he shouldn't say.
N'when he's nothing else to do
  He swell up like he'd like to bust,
N'pounds on something with his fist
N'tells us 'bout some wicked trust.
  I always wondered why that was —
    I guess it's cause
    Taft never does.

He tells the farmers how to sow
N'shows the cav'lry how to ride,
N'if you try to say a word
  He's angry, n'he says you lied.
N'when it's quiet over here
  He goes way far acrost the seas
N'gets a great big gun n'shoots
  The elephants n'chimpanzees.
  I always wondered why that was —
    I guess it's cause
    Taft never does.

— EUGENE O'NEILL.

(September 2, 1912)

## (Untitled)

All night I lingered at the Beach
And trod the board walk up and down —
I vainly sought to cop a peach.

I had prepared a charming speach,
To woo the fair ones of the town —
All night I lingered at the Beach.

Quoth I "Sweet damsel I beseach
That you will smile on me", poor clown!
I vainly sought to cop a peach.

With the persistence of a leach,
I clung to every passing gown —
All night I lingered at the Beach.

I swore my love to all, but each
Passed me the haughty freezing frown —
I vainly sought to cop a peach.

I prayed to all, both white and brown —
They only "kicked my dog aroun".
All night I lingered at the Beach —
I vainly sought to cop a peach.

—E. O.

(September 6, 1912)

## TO A BULL MOOSE

(With apologies to Bobby Burns)

Braw, snortin, roarin, fearsome beastie
What a tumult's in thy breastie
Thou needna think that we will heed thee
    Or mark thy clatter
Thou canna make us believe we need thee
    By inane chatter.

Poor beastie, t'is an ill opinion
To think we'd suffer thy dominion
Thy fate is sealed for next November
    After election
Then present boasts thou will remember
    With deep dejection.

So, Moosie, cease thy bragging vain
We canna hear thee wi'out pain
The best laid plans of Moose and men
    Gang aft agley
We can but hope that thine will wend
    The self-same way.
                —E. O.

(September 11, 1912)

### (Untitled)

I might forget the subway guard
   Who said "Please watch your step" to me
The silent barber once I met
   Might e'en escape my memory
But I shall surely ne'er forget
   While breath of life is left in me
The waiter who urbanely said
   "I really can't accept a fee."

                — E. O.

(September 11, 1912)

## (Untitled)

I used to ponder deeply o'er
The referendum and recall.
And culled statistics evermore
About the mighty tariff wall.

I followed every candidate,
Read their acceptance speeches, too,
And went to hear them all orate
'Bout what they would or wouldn't do.

As I have said, my thoughts flew high,
(They very rarely touched the ground.)
So that I was considered by
My friends as being most profound.

But truth will out; I must confess
At present I am in a fix.
Although my mind's uneasiness
Has naught to do with politics.

You tell me that the G. O. P.
Has cleaned up in the state of Maine?
Hush! hush! what matters it to me?
But say, who'll cop that opening game?

Will Wood last out? Will Marquard blow?
Is Matty still there with the science?
Can Speaker wallop Jeff Tesreau?
In brief, which is it, Sox or Giants?

—E. G. O'Neill.

(September 13, 1912)

## NOCTURNE

The sunset gun booms out in hollow roar
  Night breathes upon the waters of the bay
  The river lies, a symphony in gray,
Melting in shadow on the further shore.

A sullen coal barge tugs its anchor chain
  A shadow sinister, with one faint light
  Flickering wanly in the dim twilight,
It lies upon the harbor like a stain.

Silence. Then through the stillness rings
  The fretful echo of a sea-gull's scream,
  As if one cried who sees within a dream
Deep rooted sorrow in the heart of things.

The cry that Sorrow knows and would complain
  And impotently struggle to express —
  Some secret shame, some hidden bitterness —
Yet evermore must sing the same refrain.

Silence once more. The air seems in a swoon
  Beneath the heavens thousand opening eyes
  While from the far horizon's edge arise
The first faint silvery tresses of the moon.

                                    — E. O'Neill.

        (September 13, 1912)

## BALLARD OF
## THE MODERN MUSIC LOVER

I have tried to fall for the stuff of Mozart
    Handel, Haydn — a dozen or more
But I guess my ear isn't framed for "beaux arts"
    For I found them all a terrible bore.
    I suffered through concerts by the score
Orgies of music that shook the room
    Till my brain was sick and my head was sore
    But the joy of my heart is a rag time tune.

I confess I'm fond of that Mendelssohn — rag
    But not of Liszt's Rhapsody Hungarian
Which sounds to me like a musical jag
    (You see I am but a rank barbarian).
    The long-haired high-brows call me "vulgarian"
When the "Great Big Beautiful Doll" I croon
    For I'm strong for the music that's real American
And the joy of my heart is a rag time tune.

You can't swing in the maze of the Turkey Trot
    To the strains of a Chopin symphony
Or the horrible noise that Wagner wrote
    Or chaotic nocturnes of Tschaikowsky
    Such spasms are much too deep for me
And I pine mid the all-pervading gloom
    To hear that song 'bout the Robert E. Lee
For the joy of my heart is a rag time tune.

Envoy

High-brows, whom classic music quickeneth
Heed well the burden of my vulgar rune,
Your lofty tumbling wearies me to death.
The joy of my heart is a rag time tune.

— E. G. O'NEILL.

(September 17, 1912)

## (Untitled)

As I scan the pages of history's scroll
  I find many scenes of woe,
And I read of the griefs that have griped the soul
  In the time of the long ago.
Of the tears and sobs at the Trojan gate,
  When the iron horse nosed in;
And the great despair of Alex the Great
  With no more games to win.
And Caesar's thoughts were gloomy and dark
  When he piped that "Et tu Brute"
And the burning sensations of Joan of Arc,
  Were doubtless most acute.
I can sympathize with King Louis too
  As he stood on the guillotine,
And Napoleon's feelings at Waterloo
  When the Prussian host was seen.

I grant you their sorrows were great and real
  But comparison makes them light
With the gloom I feel as I ride my wheel
  To work on a Sunday night.
                              — E. O'NEILL.

(September 23, 1912)

## ONLY YOU

We walk down the crowded city street
   Thus, silently side by side
We loiter where mirth and misery meet
   In an ever refluent tide.

You thrill with the joy of the passing throng
   Or echo it's weary sighs
You gaze at each face as it hurries along
   — But I only see your eyes —

I only see your eyes, my love,
   I only see your eyes
For happiness or misery
   Are only real when seen by me
Reflected in your eyes.

We walk down the crowded city street
   Lingeringly, side by side
You throb with the city's ceaseless beat
   While I in a dream abide.

For how can its harsh triumphant din
   Make me shudder or rejoice?
When the only sound in the dream I'm in
   Is the music of your voice.

The music of your voice, my love
   The music of your voice.
The world's vibrating symphony
   Seems vague and most unreal to me
I only hear your voice.

—E. G. O'NEILL.

(September 27, 1912)

## "IT'S GREAT WHEN YOU GET IN"

Sept. 28, 1912. Previously Published in B. H. Clark's
"Eugene O'Neill."

## THE SHUT-EYE CANDIDATE

(W. A. To Rudyard Kipling)

Sez the wily campaign manager
    To the Corporations' man,
"Our candidate has gone dead broke,
    So help him if you can.
For the tour is long and the speeches strong
    And travelling comes high,
And we'll have to gather the coin in
    In order to get by."

Then it's "Graft!!! What graft?" we can't see anything wrong,
    Standard Oil and U. S. Steel, but candidate shut your eye;
And it's "Pass! All's well!" as the coin rolls along,
    You'll need an affidavit pretty badly by-and-by.

"It's private cars on the railroads
    A'roaming the country wide,
It's hotel bills and other ills
    And a helluvalot beside.
Don't throw your chip in boldly
    Be as cagey as you can,
For our candidate, be it understood,
    Is a conscientious man."

Then it's "Graft! What graft?" as we gather up the tin,
  Swift, Cudahy and Armour, O candidate shut your eye,
And it's "Pass! All's well!" as the old long green comes in,
  But you'll need an affidavit pretty badly by-and-by.

                              —Eugene O'Neill.

        (October 3, 1912)

## LOVE'S LAMENT

(Tigean Te Oa'Neill)

There ain't no nothing much no more,
   And nothin' ain't no use to me;
In vain I pace the lonely shore,
   For I have saw the last of thee.

I seen a ship upon the deep
   And signalled this here fond lament:
"I haven't did a thing but weep
   Since thou hast went."

Alas! fur I ain't one of they,
   What hasn't got no faith in love.
And them fond words of yesterday
   They was spoke true, by heaven above!

Is it all off twixt I and you?
   Will you go and wed some other gent?
The things I done, I'd fain undo,
   Since thou hast went.

O Love! I done what I have did,
   Without no thought of no offense
Return, return, I sadly bid
   Before my feelings get intense.

I have gave up all wealth and show
   I have gave up all thought of fame,
But, oh! what joy 'twould be to know
   That thou hadst came!
                  — "Contributed."

     (October 16, 1912)

## "THE QUEST OF THE GOLDEN GIRL"

I wandered the wide world over and lingered in many a land in vain appeal for my great ideal, the girl who could understand. I looked over the queens of Paris, of London and Berlin too, but they simply couldn't get hep to me so I beat it over the blue. I made mad love to an Esquimau as we froze on the bergs of Svork, and earned headaches at Irish wakes a'courting colleens in Cork. I tied up with a South Sea Islander, but little hampered by clothes, and fell for a peach in Somaliland with a shin bone through her nose. I sauntered through South America from Caracas to the Horn. Most passionate flames were the Latin dames and I barely weathered the storm. I snared the fairy Geisha in tea rooms of Tokio and a slant-eyed "Chink" was the next I think fell a victim to Cupid's bow. My next was a Moro damsel who called me the "soul of her life" but I blew in fear cause the little dear was so handy with her knife. I followed my quest to Africa from Cairo to the Cape, squeezed many a hand in many a land with many a narrow escape. Ever the heart of me hungered, till I suddenly ceased to roam, and stowed away one lonely day on a boat that sailed for home. And there I finally met her and asked her to be my wife, and she understood as I knew she would the cause of my yearning strife. She revealed to me my longing in words no one could shirk when she said "My dear, my income's clear and you won't have to work."

—E. G. O'NEILL.

(October 17, 1912)

## THE GLINTS OF THEM

Laughing, gift laden did they come to me,
Their hands made fair with wonderous silver hours,
Their hair encrowned with wreaths of memory.
Light loves of old, as fragile as the flowers
Star-dotted in the gloom of woodland ways —
   Gold summer days.

The drowsy heated noontide reverie;
Fantastic dreams beneath the lonely moon;
The weary sobbing rythm of the sea,
Sighing its even melancholy rune;
The sand that shudders in the sun's hot rays —
   Gold summer days.

The bright, green lawns that lean down to the bay;
The dancing, eerie heat waves on the road;
Cool shade wherein my listless feet would stray
Beneath great trees, the lovely nymph's abode
Or haunted by the fairy ghosts of fays —
   Gold summer days.

The sullen vessel straining at its chain;
The pungent smell of oily pitch and tow;
A vista of strange lands seen once again,
A breath of memory from the long ago;
The longing song of fortune's castaways —
   Gold summer days.

             — E. G. O'NEILL.

(October 19, 1912)

## HITTING THE PIPE

"When my dreams come true — when my dreams
come true — I shall lean out from my casement
in the starlight and the dew" — J. W. Riley.

When my dreams come true — when my dreams come true —
I'll be sitting in the office here with nothing else to do
But to write a comic story or to spin a little rhyme,
I won't have to do rewriting, I'll have lots of leisure time
For to sit and chatter politics and dream the whole night
    through,
I will never cover socials when my dreams come true!

When my dreams come true I will never stoop to read
The proof of advertisements telling people what they need.
I will only write the stories that are sure to make a hit,
And the mighty city editor will never cut a bit,
But put them in just as they are and compliment me, too,
I'll be the star reporter when my dreams come true.

When my dreams come true there will not be a mistake
In a single line of copy that the linotypers make
I will never have to count the letters framing up a head
And every night at twelve o'clock will find me home in bed
I will shun the railroad station and the police station, too,
And only cover prize fights when my dreams come true.

When my dreams come true all my comments wise and sage
Will be featured double column on the editor's own page
Personals will be no object, I won't have to go and hunt
The history of the tug-boats that infest the water-front
Fire alarms may go to blazes, suicides and murders too,
I'll be editing Laconics when my dreams come true.

—E. G. O'NEILL.

(October 22, 1912)

## SENTIMENTAL STUFF

I wrote a sonnet to her eyes,
   In terms Swinburnian and erotic;
Poured out the burden of my sighs
   With language lurid and exotic —
      She did not heed.

I wrote a ballard I deemed fair
   With sprightly play of silver rhyme
To sing her glorious golden hair
   Aglow with sun in summer time —
      She did not hear.

I wrote a soulful villanelle
   About the wonder of her mouth,
Lips like the crimson flowers that dwell
   In forests of the tropic south —
      She made no sign.

I wrote a musical rondeau
   To praise her roguish little nose,
Dabbed at with powder, white as snow,
   Through which a freckle warmly glows —
      She would not see.

I wrote a solemn, stately ode,
   Lauding her matchless symmetry,
I thought that this might be a road
   To open up her heart to me —
      She spoke no word.

Then in a feeble triolette,
  I told the keenness of her wit;
A blush of anger o'er me crept
  I was so much ashamed of it —
    — She fell for it —

    — And this is it —
"What matters it if you are fair?
  I love you for your wit,
Your mental poise, your wisdom rare,
  What matters it if you are fair?
Beauty is fleeting, light as air
  I'll naught to do with it,
What matters it if you are fair?
  I love you for your wit."

She praised this assininity
  And scorned the good ones that I wrote,
This bunch of femininity,
  On whom my fond affections dote —
    Has got my goat.

She put my real ones on the pan,
  And gave my puerile one a puff,
And said, "I'll love you if you'll can
  That horrid sentimental stuff —
    I've had enough."

                    — E. G. O'NEILL.

    (October 28, 1912)

## A REGULAR SORT OF A GUY

He fights where the fighting is thickest
  And keeps his high honor clean;
From finish to start, he is sturdy of heart,
  Shunning the petty and mean;
With his friends in their travail and sorrow,
  He is ever there to stand by,
And hark to their plea, for they all know that he
  Is a regular sort of a guy.

He cheers up the sinner repentant
  And sets him again on his feet;
He is there with a slap, and a pat on the back,
  For the lowliest bum on the street;
He smiles when the going is hardest,
  With a spirit no money can buy;
And take it from me, we all love him 'cause he
  Is a regular sort of a guy.

I don't care for the praise of the nations,
  Or a niche in the great hall of fame,
Or that posterity should remember me
  When my dust and the dust are the same;
But my soul will be glad if my friends say
  As they turn from my bier with a sigh
"Though he left no great name, yet he played out the game
  Like a regular sort of a guy."

— E. G. O'NEILL.

(November 4, 1912)

## THE LONG TALE

(With apologies to R. K.)

There's a speech within the hall, echoes back from wall to wall,
    Where the campaign banners swing;
And the voters sit so patient, listening to the tale so ancient,
    That the old spell binders sing.
You have heard the story of thieving Trusts
    And their lawless lust for gain;
You have heard that song — how long! how long?
    T'is the same old tale again!
We have fallen for that same bull, dear lass,
    Many a season through,
Till we're getting fed up with the old tale, the cold tale, thrice
      told tale.
Yes, we're just about sick of that Long Tale, the tale that is
      never new.

It's North you may run to Seattle, Washington,
    Or South to the Florida strait;
Or East all the way to Massachusetts Bay,
    Or West to the Golden Gate;
And the greatest bluffs hold good, dear lass,
    And the wildest tale seems true,
And the men talk big on the old tale, the cold tale, thrice told
      tale.
Yes, lies run large on the Long Tale, the tale that is never new.

The voters are grown cold, and the campaign's growing old,
    And the speakers shout o'er the land;
Every candidate will bust, every blooming wicked Trust,
    At least, so we're made to understand.
For election's drawing near, dear lass,
    And the orator's face is blue.
So harken again to the old tale, the cold tale, thrice told tale.
Yes, try to believe in the Long Tale, the tale that is never new.

They must herd their flock of goats, they are looking for the
        votes,
    And they'll pledge you to the wide, blue sky;
They will throw the corrupt, in a manner most abrupt,
    That is, if elected — bye and bye!
O, it's wonderful stuff to pull, dear lass,
    And almost believe in it too;
They can't be stopped on the old tale, the cold tale, thrice told
        tale.
They're hard to beat on the Long Tale, the tale that is never
        new.

O the big parades at night, with the torches flying bright,
    And the brazen blare of the band;
When the voter walks and walks, and the speaker talks and talks,
    Placing his rivals on the pan;
And he's sure to spiel on the Trust, dear lass,
    That's a thing he can't fail to do,
When he opens his mouth for the old tale, the cold tale, thrice
        told tale.
When he bangs his fist in the Long Tale, the tale that is never
        new.

O the murmur of the crowd, and the cheering long and loud,
  As the candidate's chest expands;
And our feelings nearly boil, as he bawls out Standard Oil,
  For crushing our freedom in its hands.
He is going to stop all that, dear lass,
  But just between me and you;
I've heard it before this old tale, the cold tale, thrice told tale.
Yes, I've had an ear full of the Long Tale, the tale that is never
      new.

Yet before he turns to go, on the tariff high and low,
  He is sure to argue a while;
Let us not have a misgiving, he will lower cost of living,
  So he assures us with a smile.

You have heard the drool of the tariff wall,
  Which the robber Trusts maintain;
You have heard that song — how long! how long?
  He's telling the tale again!

Lord knows what he'd find to say, dear lass,
  And the Deuce knows what he would do
If he couldn't fall back on the old tale, the cold tale, thrice told
      tale.
If he couldn't bull on the Long Tale, the tale that is never new.

                    — Eugene Gladstone O'Neill.

          (November 5, 1912)

## THE CALL

I have eaten my share of "stock fish"
  On a steel Norwegian bark;
With hands gripped hard to the royal yard
  I have swung through the rain and the dark.
I have hauled upon the braces
  And bawled the chanty song,
And the clutch of the wheel had a friendly feel,
  And the Trade Wind's kiss was strong.

So it's back to the sea, my brothers,
  Back again to the sea.
I'm keen to land on a foreign strand
  Back again to the sea.

I have worked with a chipping hammer
  And starved on a lime-juice tramp.
While she plunged and rolled, I have cleaned the hold
  Or coughed in the bilges damp.
I have sweated a turn at trimming,
  And faced the stoke-hold's hell,
And strained my ear in attempt to hear .
  The relieving watch's bell.

So it's back to the sea, my brothers,
  Back again to the sea.
And where I'll go, I don't quite know —
  Just back again to the sea.

For it's grand to lie on the hatches
   In the glowing tropic night
When the sky is clear and the stars seem near
   And the wake is a trail of light,
And the old hulk rolls so softly
   On the swell of the southern sea
And the engines croon in a drowsy tune
   And the world is mystery!
So it's back to the sea, my brothers,
   Back again to the sea.
Where regrets are dead and blood runs red,
   Back again to the sea.

Then it's ho! for the moonlit beaches,
   Where the palm trees dip and sway,
And the noontide heat in the sleeping street
   Where the restless burros bray.
I can hear the bands on the plazas
   In towns of a far-off land,
And the words come strong of a deep sea song,
   "We're bound for the Rio Grande".

So it's back to the sea, my brothers,
   Back again to the sea.
Where white seas toss 'neath the Southern Cross,
   Back again to the sea.

I'm sick of the land and landsmen
And pining once more to roam,
For me there is rest on the long waves crest
Where the Red Gods make their home.
There's a star on the far horizon
And a smell in the air that call,
And I cannot stay for I must obey
So good-bye, good luck to you all!

So it's back to the sea, my brothers,
Back again to the sea.
Hear the seagulls cry as the land lights die!
Back again to the sea.

—E. G. O'NEILL.

(November 19, 1912)

## SONNETS

*The Haymarket.*

The music blares into a rag-time tune —
　　The dancers whirl around the polished floor;
Each powdered face a set expression wore
　　Of dull satiety, and wan smiles swoon
On rouged lips at sallies opportune
　　Of maudlin youths whose sodden spirits soar
On drunken wings; while through the opening door
　　A chilly blast sweeps like the breath of doom.

In sleek dress suit an old man sits and leers
　　With vulture mouth and blood-shot, beady eyes
At the young girl beside him. Drunken tears
　　Fall down her painted face, and choking sighs
Shake her, as into his familiar ears
　　She sobs her sad, sad history — and lies!

　　　　　　　　　　　　— E. G. O'NEILL.

*Noon.*

'Tis noon, the fitful sunlight feebly gleams
　　Thro' hurrying clouds with dull uncertainty.
Distorted shadows in strange fantasy
　　Play like vague phantoms wandering in dreams
Upon the shivering surface of the streams.
　　The trees sway to and fro protestingly
Dancing as if to the weird melody
　　Of anguished protest that the north wind screams.

The seer, dead leaves whirl in confusion by,
  Fleeing as if from nameless pestilence.
A solitary hawk up in the sky
  Floats on the wind in peaceful indolence,
Like some old God, who from Olympus high
  Looks on our dull world with indifference.

—E. G. O'NEILL.

(November 21, 1912)

## BALLARD OF THE SEAMY SIDE

Where is the lure of the life you sing?
  Let us consider the seamy side:
The fo'castle bunks and the bed bugs' sting,
  The food that no stomach could abide,
The crawling "salt horse" flung overside
  And the biscuits hard as a cannon ball;
What fascinations can such things hide?
  "They're part of the game and I loved it all."

Think of the dives on the water front
  And the drunken brutes in dungaree,
Of the low dance halls where the harpies hunt
  And the maudlin seaman so carelessly
Squanders the wages of months at sea
  And maybe is killed in a bar room brawl;
The spell of these things explain to me —
  "They're part of the game and I loved it all."

Tell me the lure of "working mail"
  With two hours sleep out of twenty four,
Hefting bags huge as a cotton bale
  Weighing a hundred pounds or more,
Till your back is bent and your shoulders sore
  And you heed not the bosun's profane call;
Such work, I should think, you must abhor!
  "It's part of the game and I loved it all."

"I grant you the feed is passing bad,
   And the labor great, and the wages small,
That the ways of a sailor on shore are mad
   But they're part of the game and I loved it all."

—E. G. O'NEILL.

(November 22, 1912)

## THE LAY OF THE SINGER'S FALL

A singer was born in a land of gold,
  In the time of long ago
And the good faries gathered from heath and wold
  With gracious gifts to bestow.
They gave him the grace of mirth and Song,
  They crowned him with Health and Joy
And love for the Right and hate for the Wrong
  They instilled in the soul of the boy;
But when they were gone, through the open door
  The Devil of Doubt crept in,
And he breathed his poison in every pore
  Of the sleeping infant's skin,
And in impish glee, said "Remember me
  For I shall abide for aye with thee
From the very first moment thine eyes shall see
  And know the meaning of sin."

The singer became a man and he fought
  With might of his pen and hand
To show for evil the cure long sought,
  And spread Truth over the land;
Till the Devil mockingly said, "In sooth
  'T is a sorry ideal you ride,
For the truth of truths is there is no truth!"
  — And the faith of the singer died —

And the singer was sad and he turned to Love
  And the arms of his ladye faire,
He sang of her eyes as the stars above
  He sang of — and kissed — her hair;
Till the Devil whispered, "I fondly trust
  This is folly and nought beside,
For the greatest of loves is merely lust!"
  — And the heart of the singer died —

So the singer turned from the world's mad strife
  And he walked in the paths untrod,
And thrilled to the dream of a future life
  As he prayed to the most high God;
Till the Devil murmured with sneering breath,
  "What think you the blind skies hide?
There is nothing sure after death but death!"
  — And the soul of the singer died —

And the lips of the singer were flecked with red
  And torn with a bitter cry,
"When Truth and Love and God are dead
  It is time, full time, to die!"
And the Devil in triumph chuckled low,
  "There is always suicide,
It's the only logical thing I know."
  — And the life of the singer died.

           — E. G. O'NEILL.

(November 27, 1912)

## TO WINTER

"Blow, blow, thou winter wind,"
   Away from here,
And I shall greet thy passing breath
   Without a tear.

I do not love thy snow and sleet
   Or icy floes;
When I must jump or stamp to warm
   My freezing toes.

For why should I be happy or
   E'en be merry
In weather only fitted for
   Cook or Perry.

My eyes are red, my lips are blue
   My ears frost bitt'n;
Thy numbing kiss doth e'en extend
   Thro' my mitten.

I am cold, no matter how I warm
   Or clothe me;
O Winter, greater bards have sung
   I loathe thee!
         —E. G. O'NEILL.

(December 9, 1912)

# INDEX

(Material in Part II has not been indexed here)

ALL GOD'S CHILLUN GOT WINGS, 43, 44, 45, 49, 51, 52, 58, 60, 82
        First Edition, 44
        First Printing, 43
        English Edition, 45
American Caravan, The, 66, 71
American Dramatist Series, 5
*American Mercury, The*
        1924, February—43, 45
American Play Co., 28, 32, 37
Anathema, 77
ANNA CHRISTIE, 36, 38, 39, 41, 44, 47, 51, 52, 58, 60, 82
        First Edition, 36
        First Separate Edition, 38
           Facsimile, 39
        English Edition, 38
        Illustrated Edition, 41
ARE THE ACTORS TO BLAME?, 43

BALLARD OF THE MODERN MUSIC LOVER, 133-134
BALLARD OF OLD GIRLS, 125-126
BALLARD OF THE SEAMY SIDE, 157-158
Bechhofer, C. E., 31, 33
BEFORE BREAKFAST, 10, 12, 13, 49, 53, 54, 56, 58, 59
       First Edition, 10
          Facsimile, 11
       First Separate Edition, 12
          Facsimile, 13
       English Edition, 59
BEYOND THE HORIZON, 23, 24, 26, 28, 30, 35, 36, 44, 47, 53, 54,
       58, 60, 82
       First Edition, 23
          Facsimile, 24
       English Edition, 26
Boni & Liveright, Inc., 17, 19, 23, 27, 28, 30, 32, 34, 35, 36, 44, 47,
       48, 50, 51, 58, 63, 70, 71, 72, 73
*Boston Evening Transcript*
       1925, October 31 — 56
BOUND EAST FOR CARDIFF, 8, 19, 32, 48, 59
       First Edition, 8
Bourne, Randolph, 15
Boyce, Neith, 10
Brooks, Van Wyck, 66
Bryant, Louise, 8
Burns, Robert, 129

Cabot Homestead, The, 46
CALL, THE, 152-154
Chris Christopherson, 23
Clark, Barrett, 32, 61, 62, 138
COLLECTED PLAYS, 47-49, 51, 51-56
          Limited Edition, 47
          Trade Edition, 51
             Facsimile, 52
Conning Tower, The, 7, 119

Contemporary One-Act Plays of 1921, 21, 22
          First Edition, 22
Cook, George Cram, 33
Copp Clark Co., The, 5

De Casseres, Benjamin, 77
Dell, Floyd, 8
DESIRE UNDER THE ELMS, 43, 45, 46, 49, 50, 53, 55, 58
          First Edition, 49
          First Separate Edition, 50
          English Edition, 45
DIFF'RENT, 28, 31, 36, 44, 47, 51, 52, 58
          First Edition, 28
DREAMY KID, THE, 21, 22, 49, 53, 55, 58, 59
          First Edition, 22
          First Printing, 21
          English Edition, 59
DYNAMO, 57, 71, 78, 79, 80, 81, 82
          First Edition, 78
               Facsimile, 81
          English Edition, 79
               Facsimile, 80
          Limited Edition, 82

EMPEROR JONES, THE, 27, 28, 29, 31, 32, 33, 34, 36, 44, 49, 53,
               55, 58, 60, 82
          First Edition, 28
               Facsimile, 29
          First Printing, 27
          English Edition, 31
          First Separate Edition, 32
               English, 33
          Illustrated Edition, 34
Ervine, St. John, 20
"Eugene O'Neill", 61, 62, 138
European Theories of the Drama, 32

Fifty Contemporary One-Act Plays, 33
FIRST MAN, THE, 36, 38, 44, 47, 53, 55, 58
        First Edition, 36
        English Edition, 38
FOG, 7
Foreword, 77
FOUNTAIN, THE, 36, 46, 58, 59
        First Edition, 58
        English Edition, 59
F. P. A., 7
FRATRICIDE, 5, 113-117
FREE, 2, 3, 111
        First Edition, 3

Game, The, 8
GLINTS OF THEM, THE, 143
GOLD, 26, 28, 35, 47, 53, 55, 56, 58
        First Edition, 35
        English Edition, 26
Goldberg, Isaac, 56
Gorham Press, The, 5
Gotham Book Mart, 77
GREAT GOD BROWN, THE, 58, 59, 60, 82
        First Edition, 58
        First Separate Edition, 60
        English Edition, 59
*Greenwich Playbill*
        1924-1925, No. 2 — 46
        1925-1926, No. 3 — 46
Greenwich Village Theatre, 46

HAIRY APE, THE, 36, 38, 40, 44, 49, 53, 55, 58, 60, 82
        First Edition, 36
        First Separate Edition, 40
        English Edition, 38
Harper & Brothers, 66

HAYMARKET, THE, 155
Hiawatha, 121
History of the American Drama, A, 65
HITTING THE PIPE, 144-145
Horace Liveright, Inc., 40, 41, 78, 82

ILE, 16, 19, 32, 48, 59
            First Edition, 19
            First Printing, 16
IN THE ZONE, 19, 48, 59
            First Edition, 19
IT'S GREAT WHEN YOU GET IN, 62, 138

Jonathan Cape Ltd., 20, 26, 31, 33, 38, 45, 59, 60, 64, 75, 79

King, Alexander, 34, 40, 41
King Arthur's Socks, 8
Kipling, Rudyard, 138, 149
Knopf, Alfred, 44
Kreymborg, Alfred, 10, 66

Laconics, 4, 121
LAZARUS LAUGHED, 66, 68, 69, 70, 71, 79, 82
            First Edition, 70
                  Facsimile, 69
            First Printing of First Act, 66
                  Facsimile, 68
            English Edition, 79
            Limited Edition, 71
LAY OF THE SINGER'S FALL, THE, 159-160
Letters, 27, 42, 43, 56, 57, 61, 62
Lima Beans, 10
LONG TALE, THE, 149-151
LONG VOYAGE HOME, THE, 15, 19, 48, 59
            First Edition, 19
            First Printing, 15

LOVE'S LAMENT, 140-141
Loving, Pierre, 33


Macaulay Co., The, 66
MARCO MILLIONS, 62, 64, 82
                First Edition, 62
                English Edition, 64
                Limited Edition, 64
*Masses, The*
                1917, February—14, 120
Mencken, H. L., 44
Modern Library, 19
Moody, William Vaughn, 66
MOON OF THE CARIBBEES, 9, 16, 17, 18, 20, 23, 25, 28, 35, 36, 40,
                44, 47, 56, 58, 59, 60, 82
                First Edition, 17
                        Facsimile, 18
                First Printing, 17
                English Edition, 20
Mumford, Lewis, 66


Nathan, George Jean, 44, 56
*New London Telegraph*
                1912, August 26—December 9,—4, 121-161
*New York Call*
                1914, May 17,—5, 117
*New York Evening Post*
                1926, February 13,—57
                        November 27,—57
                1929, February 9,—57
*New York Times*
                1920, April 11,—27
                1921, December 18,—27
*New York Tribune*
                1915, July 5,—7, 119

*New York World*
    1929, February 10,—78
NOCTURNE, 132
NOON, 155-156

Ole Devil, The, 28
ONLY YOU, 136-137

Playwright's Theatre, 8
PLAYS, COLLECTED, 47-49, 51-56
Pleiades Club Year Book, 2, 3, 112
    First Edition, 3
      Facsimile, 2
Poems, Untitled, 127, 128, 130, 131, 135
Provincetown-Greenwich Plays, 50
*Provincetown Playbill*
    1923-1924, No. 1—42
    1924-1925, No. 5—43
    1925-1926, No. 1—43
Provincetown Players, 8, 10, 14, 28, 32
Provincetown Playhouse, 42
Provincetown Plays, The, 8, 10, 11, 20
    First Series, 8
    Third Series, 10
      Facsimile, 11

"QUEST OF THE GOLDEN GIRL", 142
Quinn, Arthur Hobson, 65

RECKLESSNESS, 7
REGULAR SORT OF A GUY, A, 148
Riley, J. W., 127, 144
Robert M. McBride & Co., 61, 62
ROPE, THE, 19, 49, 59
    First Edition, 19
Rosenfeld, Paul, 66

*Seven Arts, The,*
        1917, June—15
SENTIMENTAL STUFF, 146-147
Shay, Frank, 8, 10, 12, 14, 21, 22, 31, 32, 33
Short Story, 15
SHUT-EYE CANDIDATE, THE, 138-139
Sketches, 43, 57, 58
*Smart Set, The*
        1917, October—15
        1918, May—16
            August—17
Sonnets, 155-156
SPEAKING, TO THE SHADE OF DANTE, OF BEATRICES, 7, 118-119
Stewart Kidd Co., 22, 27, 30, 32
Stieglitz, Alfred, 67
STRANGE INTERLUDE, 72, 73, 74, 75, 76, 82
        First Edition, 72
        English Edition, 75
        Limited Edition, 73
            Facsimile, 74
        "Extracts from — —", 76
STRAW, THE, 28, 31, 35, 36, 44, 49, 53, 54, 56, 58
        First Edition, 28
SUBMARINE, 14, 120

*Theatre Arts Magazine*
        1920, January—21, 23
        1921, January—27, 30
Theatre of George Jean Nathan, 56
THIRST, 5, 6
        First Edition, 5
Tigean Te Oa'Neill, 140
TO A BULL MOOSE, 129
TOMORROW, 15
TO WINTER, 161
Two Sons, The, 10

VILLANELLE OF YE YOUNG POET'S VILLANELLE, 124

War and The Intellectuals, The, 15
WARNINGS, 7
Washington Square Bookshop, 9, 12, 14
WATERWAYS CONVENTION, THE, 121-123
WEB, THE, 7
WELDED, 44, 45, 49, 53, 55, 56, 58
          First Edition, 44
          English Edition, 45
WHERE THE CROSS IS MADE, 19, 49, 59
          First Edition, 19
WORKS, COLLECTED, 47-49, 51-56

Zorach, William, 9, 12